B. F. Craig

The Rough Diamond

B. F. Craig

The Rough Diamond

ISBN/EAN: 9783743326903

Manufactured in Europe, USA, Canada, Australia, Japa

Cover: Foto ©ninafisch / pixelio.de

Manufactured and distributed by brebook publishing software (www.brebook.com)

B. F. Craig

The Rough Diamond

THE ROUGH DIAMOND

E. T. CRAIG

TO THE RISING GENERATION THIS BOOK IS AFFECTIONATELY DEDICATED BY

THE AUTHOR.

CONTENTS.

The Story of a Hundred Years. Pen Pictures of Eventful Scenes and Struggles of Life.

	Page.
Scene 1—Introduction	9
Scene 2—The Hero of Shirt-Tail Bend	18
Scene 3—The Separated Sisters	27
Scene 4—Roxie Daymon and Rose Simon	39
Scene 5—The Belle of Port William	50
Scene 6—The Second Generation	62
Scene 7—War Between the States	77

History, Science, Philosophy and Art, Blended in Original Lectures.

Lecture 1—On Liberty and Law	93
Lecture 2—On Time and Motion	106
Lecture 3—On Mind and Organism	121
Lecture 4—On Man and Animals	138
Lecture 5—On Spirit and Soul	156

CONTENTS.

GENIUS AND POETRY.

Genius 175
My Native Land—address to Young America . . . 176
Rise and Fall of Old Nick—to the Devil 180
Confederate Flag—to the Ladies of Plattsburg . . 183
Family and Fate—to a Female Relative 184
Twilight—Intermediate Body and Soul 187
The Devil and Tom Walker—a Dialogue 188
The Beautiful Snow—an Emblem of Virtue 192
The Workmen's Saturday Night—a Tribute to Honest Labor 196
Inside View of the United States Mail—Revealed by the Angel of Observation 198
Hard Times 202
The Power of Truth 204
The Wheels of Time 204
The Days of My Childhood 205
Ideas and Idols—Essay on Jacob and Laban . . . 206
The Dying Drunkard to His Soul 208
The Moneyless Man vs. Moneyless Woman 211
The Poet vs. Tom Watson's Deer 213

Pen Pictures.

Of Eventful Scenes and Struggles of Life.

SCENE FIRST—INTRODUCTION.

It is fashionable to preface what we have to say.

Some men build a large portico in front of the edifice they erect.

This may attract the eye of a stranger, but no real comfort can be realized until we enter the house.

And then no display of fine furniture or studied form of manners can equal a whole-soul, hearty welcome.

Besides, no long proclamation of the entertainment can equal in interest the entertainment itself.

Without further preliminary ceremony, I will introduce you to the sad experience of a living man:—

Born in the house of respectable parents, on the southern bank of the beautiful Ohio, in the dawn of the nineteenth century, and educated in a log school house, the first scenes of my manhood were upon the waters of the great Mississippi river and its tributaries. Leaving home at an early age, no hopeful boy was ever turned loose in the wide world more ignorant of the traps and pit-falls set to catch and degrade the youth of this broad and beautiful land.

At Vicksburg, Natchez, Under-the-Hill, and the Crescent City, with armies of dissipation—like the Roman Cæsar—I came, I saw, I conquered.

I had been taught from my earliest infancy that a *thief* was a scape-goat—on the left-hand side of the left gate, where all the goats are to be crowded on the last day. *And that saved me.*

For I soon discovered that the *gambler* and the *thief* acted upon the same *theory.*

Having no desire to live through the scenes of my life again—I am not writing my own history, but the history of some of the events in the lives of others that I have witnessed or learned by tradition—in the execution of the task I shall enter the palace like the log cabin—without stopping to ring the bell.

Although I have been a diligent reader for more than forty years, my greatest knowledge of human character has been drawn from observation. For prudential reasons some fancy names are used in this story, but the characters drawn are true to the letter. Local, it is true, but may they not represent character throughout this broad continent? In 1492 Columbus discovered America—a Rough Diamond—a New World.

Our fathers passed through the struggle of life in the *rough*, and the log cabin ought to be as dear to the American heart as the modern palace. Emancipated from ideas of locality, I hope, and honestly trust that the sentiments in the Rough Diamond will be treasured in the hearts of the millions of my countrymen, and that no American character will ever become so brilliant that it cannot allude with a nat've pride to the Rough Diamond—our country a hundred years ago.

And with a thousand other ideas brought to the mind, and blended with the Rough Diamond, may the good Angel of observation rest with the reader as you peruse these pages.

Near the seat of the present town of Helena, Arkansas,

old Billy Horner and Henry Mooney made a race on two little ponies, called respectively Silver Heels and the Spotted Buck.

The distance was one quarter of a mile, and the stake one hundred dollars.

Wishing to obtain the signature of the Governor of Arkansas to a land grant and title to a certain tract of land on the Mississippi river, I determined to attend the races.

The ponies were to start at twelve o'clock, on the 15th day of May. I forget the year, but it was soon after the inauguration of steam navigation on the Mississippi.

On the 14th day of May I left Bush Bayou, twenty miles below Helena and fifteen miles back from the river, where I was on a tour of surveying, in company of two negro boys, from fifteen to twenty years of age, to assist me. Our route was down the Bayou, which was evidently an old bed of the great river. How long since the muddy and turbulent waters had left this location and sought the present channel no human calculation could tell. Trees had grown up as large as any in other localities in the Mississippi bottoms, in some places extending entirely across the Bayou; in other places there was an open space one hundred yards wide and sometimes a mile long, but there were many places where the timber extended from shore to shore for miles. In such places our only guide was a blaze upon the trees, made by the first navigators of the Bayou. We started in a canoe, eight feet long and eighteen inches wide, with a large trunk, a number of tools, and three men. When all were on board the top of our boat was only three-quarters of an inch above the water. In this critical condition the negroes had to go as freight, for they are proverbially too awkward to manage a nice thing. Near the close of our journey we were attacked by an alligator. He was sixteen feet long, and larger than our boat. His attack frightened the negroes so badly that it was impossible to keep them still, and we came very near being upset. I fired several times at the alligator, with a double-barreled shot-gun, charged with twenty-four buckshot, but the shot only glanced from his scales and fell into the water. At last, frightened by the loud cries of the negroes, the animal left us.

When we arrived on the bank of the Mississippi the Western hemisphere had blindfolded the eye of day; the river was bank full, the turbulent waters bearing a large quantity of drift wood down the stream. Upon the Arkansas shore there was no sign of civilization. On the Mississippi shore, two miles below, there was a cabin, and the faint light of the inmates was the only sign of civilization that met our view. To cross the great river, in the dark, with its turbulent waters and drift wood, with a barque so heavily laden, was worse than the encounter with the alligator. I was young, brave and enthusiastic. Directing the negroes to place themselves in the bottom of the boat, and not to stir hand or foot at the risk of being knocked overboard with the paddle, I headed our little barque for the light in the cabin, which gave us a course quartering down stream. To have held her square across the stream, she would have undoubtedly filled with water. The night was dark, but the air was still as the inaudible breath of time.

Knowing that the perils of the sea, without wind, are abated one hundred fold, I made the venture, and landed safely at the Mississippi cabin.

Eighteen miles below Helena, and on the opposite side of the river, I passed the night, with a determination to be on the race ground the next day at twelve o'clock. I was up early in the morning. As I passed out the cot of my friend, in front of me the great father of waters rolled on in his majesty to the bosom of the ocean.

On the background the foliage of the forest cast a green

shade upon the gray light of the morning. Every animal on the premises had sought refuge in the cane brakes from the ravages of the green-head fly and the gallinipper. Like Richard the Third—I was ready to cry, a horse—a horse—my kingdom for a horse.

Through the dim distance, half concealed by the cane, I discovered a mule, and was fortunate enough to bridle him. He was an old mule; some said the first Chickasaw Frenchman that ever settled in St. Louis rode him from the north of Mexico to the Mississippi river.

Others said that he was in the army of the First Napoleon, and had been imported across the water. Be this as it may, he was a good saddle mule, for I arrived upon the race ground fifteen minutes ahead of time.

I obtained the desired signature and saw the Spotted Buck win the race. But many said it was a jockey race, and that Silver Heels was the fleetest horse. The races continued through the evening. I had no desire to bet, but if I had, I should have bet on the fast man and not the fast horse

After this event, and nearly half a century ago, I was standing on the street in Vicksburg. It was early in the morning, and the city unusually quiet. My attention was attracted in the direction of the jail by women running indoors and men rushing along the street; I saw sticks, stones, and bricks flying, and men running as in pursuit of some wild animal, and as I caught a glimpse of the figure of the retreating man, the sharp sound of a rifle gun rang out upon the morning air.

Following on to a spot on the street where a large crowd of men had collected, I saw the face of a dead man as the body was being turned over by one of the bystanders. The lineaments of the cold, marble face, spoke in a language not to be mistaken—that the dead was, in life, a *brave man.*

I soon learned that the name of the dead man was "Alonzo Phelps," and that he had been tried for the crime of murder and sentenced by the court to be hanged by the neck until he was dead, and this was the day for his execution; that he had broken, or found an opportunity to leave the jail, and nothing would stop him but the rifle-gun in the hands of an officer of the law.

I also learned that he had written a confession of his crimes, the manuscript of which was then in the jail, for he had knocked the keeper down with a stone ink-stand, with which he had been furnished to write his confession.

By the politeness of the jailor I was permitted to examine the confession, which closed with these remarkable words, *"To-morrow is the day appointed for my execution, but I will not hang."*

The confession was afterward published. I read it many times, but have forgotten most of it. I remember he said the first man he ever murdered was in Europe, and that he was compelled, for safety, to flee the country and come to America. There was nothing so unusual in this, but the manner in which he disposed of his victim was singular, and more particularly the revelation he gave of his thoughts at the time.

He said he carried the body to a graveyard, and, with a spade that had been left there, he shoveled all of the dirt out of a newly-made grave until he came to the coffin. He then laid the body of the murdered man on the coffin and refilled the grave. "I then," says he, "left the graveyard, and spent the balance of the night in reflections. How strange, I thought, it would be for two spirits, on the last day, to find themselves in the same grave." "I thought," says he, "if the relatives of the rightful owner of the grave should, in after years, conclude to move the bones of their kinsman, when they dug them up there would be two skulls, four arms, and so on, and how it would puzzle them to get the bones of their kinsman."

After reading this confession I regretted very much that I had never seen Alonzo Phelps while living, for there was blended in his composition many strange elements. But that part of his confession that gives interest to our story was the papers taken from the man he murdered in Europe, of which we have spoken. He concealed the papers, in a certain place, on the night he buried the man, and, as he was compelled to flee the country, said papers were, a long time afterward, discovered by reading his confession made in America.

With the settlement of the West, the navigation of the western waters was one of the principal industries. Keel and flat bottom boats were the first used. Keel boats were propelled against the stream with long poles, placed with one end on the bottom of the stream and a man's shoulder at the other end, pushing the boat from under him, and consequently against the stream. Flat bottom boats only drifted with the current, sometimes bearing large cargoes.

Louisville, Kentucky, was one of the principal points between Pittsburg and New Orleans. Here the placid waters of the beautiful river rushed madly over some ledges of rocks, called the falls of Ohio. Many reshipments in an early day were performed at this point, and if the boat was taken over the falls her pilot for the trip to New Orleans was not considered competent to navigate the falls. Resident pilots, in Louisville, were always employed to perform this task.

And few of the early boatmen were ever long upon the river without having acquaintances in Louisville.

Beargrass creek emptied its lazy waters into the Ohio at a point called, at the time of which we write, the suburbs of Louisville.

In a long row of cottages on the margin of Beargrass creek, that has long since given place to magnificent buildings, was the home of a friend with whom I was stopping.

Rising early one morning, I found the neighborhood in great excitement; a woman was missing. It was Daymon's wife. She had no relatives known to the people of Louisville. She was young, intelligent, and as pure from any stain of character as the beautiful snow.

Daymon was also young. He was a laborer, or boat hand, frequently assisting in conducting boats across the falls. But he was *dissipated*, and in fits of intoxication frequently abused his wife.

All who knew Daymon's wife were ready to take the dark fiend by the throat who had consigned her beautiful form to the dark waters of Beargrass creek.

Every one was busy to find some sign or memento of the missing woman.

A large crowd had gathered around a shop, where a large woden boot hung out for a sign—a shoe shop. When I arrived on the spot a workman was examining a shoe, and testified that it was one of a pair he had previously made for Daymon's wife. The shoe had been picked up, early that morning, on the margin of Beargrass creek. Suspicion pointed her finger at Daymon, and he was arrested and charged with drowning his wife in Beargrass creek.

Daymon was not a bad-looking man, and, as the evidence was all circumstantial, I felt an uncommon interest in the trial, and made arrangements to attend the court, which was to sit in two weeks.

On the morning of the trial the court room was crowded. The counsel for the state had everything ready, and the prisoner brought to the bar. The indictment was then read, charging the prisoner with murder in the first degree. And to the question, are you guilty or not guilty? Daymon answered *not guilty*, and resumed his seat. Silence now prevailed for a few minutes, when the judge inquired, "is the state ready?" The attorney answered, "yes." The judge inquired, "has the prisoner any one to defend him?" Daymon shook his head.

"It is then the duty of the court to appoint your defense," said the judge, naming the attorneys, and the trial proceeded. The witnesses for the state being sworn, testified to the shoe as already described. In the mean time Beargrass creek had been dragged, and the body of a woman found. The fish had eaten the face beyond recognition, but a chintz calico dress was sworn to by two sewing women as identical to one they had previously made for Daymon's wife.

The state's attorney pictured all of this circumstantial evidence to the jury in an eloquence seldom equaled.

But, who ever heard a lawyer plead the cause of a moneyless man? The attorneys appointed to defend Daymon preserved only their respectability in the profession.

And the jury returned their verdict *guilty.* Nothing now remained but to pronounce the sentence, and then the execution.

The judge was a crippled man, and slowly assumed an erect position. Then casting his eyes around the court room, they rested upon the prisoner, *and he paused a moment.* That moment was silent, profound, awful! for every ear was open to catch the first sound of that sentence. The silence was broken by a wild scream at the door. The anxious crowd opened a passage, and a woman entered the court room, her hair floating upon her shoulders, and her voice wild and mellow as the horn of resurrection. That woman was Daymon's wife.

SCENE SECOND. — THE HERO OF SHIRT-TAIL BEND.

> Two boys in one house grew up side by side,
> By the mother loved, and the father's pride
> With raven locks and rosy cheeks they stood,
> As living types of the family blood.
> Don, from the mother did his mettle take,
> Dan, the Prodigal—born to be a rake.

In the month of May, 1816, the Enterprise landed at Louisville, having made the trip from New Orleans in twenty-five days. She was the first steamboat that ever ascended the Mississippi river. The event was celebrated with a public dinner, given by the citizens of Louisville to Captain Henry M. Shreve, her commander.

A new era was inaugurated on the western waters, yet the clouds of monopoly had to be blown away, and the free navigation of the Mississippi heralded across the land.

The startling events of the times are necessarily connected with our story.

For the truth of history was never surpassed by fiction, only in the imagination of weak minds.

Sixty miles above Louisville, on the southern bank of the Ohio, stood a round-log cabin, surrounded by heavy timber. In the background a towering clift reared its green-covered brow to overlook the valley—the woodland scenery seemed to say: "here is the home of the wolf and the wild cat," and it gave the place a lonesome look.

A passing neighbor had informed the inmates of the cabin that a *saw-mill* was coming up the river. Two barefooted boys stood in the front yard, and looked with hopeful eyes upon the wonder of the passing steamer. The gentle breeze that waved their infant locks, whispered the coming storms of the future.

It was the Washington, built by Captain Shreve, and was subsequently seized for navigating the western waters. The case was carried to the Supreme Court of the United States, where the exclusive pretensions of the monopolist to navigate the western waters by steam were denied.

Some of the old heroes who battled for the free navigation of the western waters, left a request to be buried on the bank of the beautiful Ohio, where the merry song of the boatman would break the stillness of their resting place, and the music of the steam engine soothe their departed spirits. Well have their desires been fulfilled.

Some long and tedious summers had passed away—notwithstanding a congressman had declared in Washington City, "that the Ohio river was frozen over six months in the year, and the balance of the season would not float a tad-pole."

The music of the steam engine on the Ohio and Mississippi rivers, had given rise to unforseen industries. Don and Dan Carlo, standing in the half-way house between boyhood and manhood, without inheriting a red cent in the wide world with which to commence the battle of life, grown up in poverty, surrounded by family pride, with willing hearts and strong arms, were ready to undertake any enterprise that glimmering fortune might point out.

A relative on the mother's side held the title papers, signed by the Governor of Arkansas, to a tract of land on the Mississippi river, who gave the privilege to Don and Dan Carlo, to establish a wood yard on said premises.

For steam navigation was not only a fixed fact, but the

boats were much improved—many of them taking on board twenty-four cords of wood at one landing

"Competition is the life of trade," and several enterprising woodmen were established in this locality; and when a passing steamboat would ring for wood after night, all anxious to show the first light, the woodmen, torch in hand, would run out of their cabins in their shirt-tails. From this circumstance, that locality was known by the boatmen from Pittsburgh to New Orleans, by the homely appellation of the *Shirt-Tail Bend*.

That, like many other localities on the Mississippi, was first settled by wood-choppers. The infantile state of society in those neighborhoods can be better imagined than described. The nearest seat of justice was forty miles, and the highest standard of jurisprudence was a *third-rate* county court lawyer. Little Rock was, perhaps, the only point in the State that could boast of being the residence of a printers' devil, or the author of a dime novel.

The wood-cutters were the representative men of the neighborhood. The Gospel of peace and good will to men was, perhaps, slightly preserved in the memories of some who had been raised in a more advanced state of civilization. The passing days were numbered by making a mark on the *day-board* every morning, and a long mark every seventh day, for the Sabbath.

Quarrels concerning property seldom, if ever, occurred. The criminal code or personal difficulties were generally settled according to the law of the early boatmen, which was: if two men had a personal quarrel, they were required to choose seconds, go ashore and fight it out. The seconds were chosen to see that no weapons were used and no foul holds were taken. It was a trial of physical strength, and when the vanquished party cried *"enough!"* the difficulty was considered settled.

I am speaking of times prior to the inauguration of the Arkansas Bowie knife and pistol Many of the early woodcutters on the Mississippi were men of sterling integrity. Don Carlo never wrote a line for the future antiquarian to ponder over, or dreamed that he was transmitting anything to posterity; yet, by his bold and noble conduct, he stamped the impress of his character upon the memories of all who witnessed the blossom of society in the woods on the Mississippi river.

Brindle Bill was a wood-chopper, but he never worked much at his profession. He was one of the class of woodcutters that were generally termed the floating part of the population. This class were employed by the proprietors of the wood yards, to cut wood by the cord—for one hundred cords they received fifty dollars.

Brindle Bill was five feet and eight inches high, with square shoulders and as strong as a buffalo—and although he was classed with the floating population, he had been in that locality for more than a year and was a shining light at *headquarters*.

This was the resort of all who claimed to be fond of fun. It was an old cabin that was built by some early backwoodsmen, who had deserted it and moved on. It was some distance from the river, and left unoccupied by the woodmen. Situated in the edge of a small cane-brake, a large quantity of cane had been cut to clear the way, and piled against the west end of the cabin.

Here the jug was kept. These men had no brilliantly lighted saloon for a resort, but human nature is the same under all circumstances. In this locality, like all others, there were two parties, or two spirits—one was to improve the other to degrade society. As we have said, Brindle Bill was the leading spirit of his party. He was always ready to fill the jug and play a social game at cards—he only bet, *as he said*, to keep up a little interest in the game. Brindle Bill always had a pocket full of money. He loved to tell long stories, and frequently related previous combats, in which he came off the victor. As the test of manhood was physical strength, Brindle Bill was the bully of the settlement—no one desired a personal quarrel with him.

Some said that S. S. Simon, the proprietor of a wood yard, sided with Brindle Bill—whether this was true or not —Simon's wife, was one of the leading spirits of the other party. She was a woman of few words, but the force of her character was felt by the whole neighborhood.

Cord, or steam wood, was the principal source of revenue, and large quantities were annually sold, thousands of dollars come into Shirt-tail Bend, but there was no improvement, they had no school house, and a church and post-office were not thought of.

Don and Dan Carlo, proprietors of one of the principal wood yards, *dear brothers*, were animated by different spirits. Dan was a fast friend of Brindle Bill. Don was a silent spirit of the other party. They were equal partners in the wood business, and when a sale was made, Dan received half of the money, but it so happened that all expenses were paid by Don. This had been the situation for a long time. In vain Don appealed to Dan—tried to arouse family pride. The two kept bachelors hall, and many times, through the long vigils of the night, Don laid before Dan, their situation, *scoffed at* by a large family relationship, because they were poor, and then representing that they must fail in their business, because half the money received would not pay expenses, to all of this, Dan would promise to reform—and promise, and promise, *and promise*, but would always fail.

In the dusk of the evening, after a large sale of wood had been made, at the Carlo wood yard, S. S. Simon, Dan Carlo, Sundown Hill and Brindle Bill were seen making their way slowly to *headquarters*. Simon's wife remarked to a person near her, "*Dan's money will go to-night.*"

Don Carlo was seen sitting alone in his cabin, his hand upon his forehead, his eyes gazing intently upon the floor. The burning coal upon the hearthstone glimmered in the glory of its element; the voice of the wild ducks upon the river shore, told the deep, dead hour of the night, and aroused Don Carlo from his reverie—the sun had crossed the meridian on the other side of the globe, and no sound of the foot-fall of his absent brother disturbed the stillness of the hour.

Don Carlo picked up a pamphlet that lay upon the table and turned over the leaves, it was the confession of *Alonzo Phelps.*

He said mentally, Phelps was a very bad, but a very brave man. He defied the city of Vicksburg, defied the law, and the State of Mississippi.

He thought of the generations before him, and family pride filled his veins with warm blood. Don Carlo was ready to face Brindle Bill, or the Brindle Devil, in defence of his rights, and he started for *headquarters.*

Cool, calculating woman — Simon's wife, the patient watcher for her absent husband, saw Don Carlo wending his way through the stillness of the night, to *headquarters.* Her keen, woman's wit, told her there was trouble ahead.

Silently, and unseen, with fire brand in hand, (this was before friction matches were thought of,) she left the Simon cabin.

When Don Carlo arrived at *headquarters,* the door and window was fastened on the inside, a faint light from a tallow candle, that glimmered through the cracks of the cabin, whispered the deep laid scheme of the inmates—S. S. Simon, Sundown Hill and Brindle Bill were banded together to swindle Dan Carlo. Don Carlo went there to enter that cabin. Quick as thought he clambered up the corner of the jutting logs, and passed down the chimney. In front of him, around a square table, sat four men. On the center of the table a large pile of shining silver dollars, enlivened the light of the tallow candle.

The players looked up in amazement; had an angel from heaven dropped among them, they would not have been more astonished. While the men sat, between doubt and fear, Don Carlo raked the money from the table, and put it in his pocket.

Brindle Bill was the first to rise from the table, he held up four cards, claimed the money, said he was personally insulted by Don Carlo, and by G—d he should fight it out. He chose S. S. Simon for his second, and boastingly prepared for the contest.

Don Carlo used no words, nor did he choose any second; Sundown Hill and Dan Carlo looked at each other, and at S. S. Simon, with a look that said, we stand by Don Carlo.

S. S. Simon hallooed *fair play*, and Brindle Bill *pitched in*. Brindle Bill was the stoutest man, Don Carlo the most active, the contest was sharp, and very doubtful, notwithstanding the boasting character of Brindle Bill, true pluck was upon the side of Don Carlo. At this critical moment, Simon's wife appeared upon the scene of action, the door of the cabin was fast, Simon was on the inside. She could hear the blows and smell the blood, for a lucky lick from Don had started the blood from Brindle Bill's nose, but could not see or know the combatants. Quick as thought, she applied the fire-brand to the cane pile, on the west end of the cabin. A strong breeze from the west soon enveloped the roof of the cabin in flames. The men rushed out into the open air much frightened. Simon's wife grabbed her husband and dragged him toward their home, with loud and eloquent cries of *shame*. The contest was ended, and Don Carlo had the money. Brindle Bill appealed to the men of his party to see that he should have *fair play*. His appeals were all in vain, the fear of him was broken, and he had no great desire to renew the contest. Seeing no hope in the future, Brindle Bill left the new settlement. And Don Carlo was justly entitled to the appellation of the *Hero of Shirt-Tail Bend*.

Society was started upon the up-grade. Some planters commenced to settle in the Bend, little towns were now springing up on the Mississippi, and Dan Carlo out of his element, made it convenient to visit the towns. A new era had dawned upon the criminal code in Arkansas—the pistol and the bowie knife, of which writers of fiction have portrayed in startling colors. Shortly after these events, Dan Carlo was found *dead in a saloon*.

It was in April, late one Saturday evening, the steamboat "Red Stone" blew up sixty-five miles above Louisville, while landing on the Kentucky shore; the boat burned to the water edge, and many lives were lost. Men returning from the South, to the homes of their nativity, were consigned to the placid waters of the Ohio for a resting place, others were mangled and torn, left to eke out a weary life, without some of their limbs. The scene upon the shore was heart-rendering above description. The body of one poor man was picked up one-quarter of a mile from the boat, in a corn field, every bone in his body was broken, and its fall to the earth made a hole in the ground, eighteen inches deep. How high he went in the air can only be conjectured, but we may safely say it was out of sight. Several were seen to fall in the middle of the river, who never reached the shore. The dead and dying were gathered up and carried to the houses nearest at hand. The inhabitants of the shore had gathered for three miles up and down the river—all classes and ages were seen pulling pieces of the wreck and struggling persons to the shore. Two girls or half-grown women passed by me walking slowly upon the pebbled shore, gazing into the water, when some distance from me, I saw one of them rush into the water up to her arm-pits and drag something to the shore. I hastened to the spot, and the girls passed on toward the wreck. Several men were carrying the apparently lifeless body of a man upon a board in the direction of the half-way castle, a place of deposit for the dead and dying. His identity was ascertained by some papers taken from his pocket, it was—Don Carlo—the "Hero of Shirt-Tail Bend."

SCENE THIRD — THE SEPARATED SISTERS.

>On the stream of human nature's blood,
>Are ups and downs in every shape and form,
>Some sail gently on a rising flood,
>And some are wrecked in a tearful storm.

Tom Fairfield was descended from one of the best families in Virginia. Yet he was animated by what we may call a *restless spirit.* He ran away from home at twelve years of age, and came to Kentucky with a family of emigrants, who settled near Boone Station, in 1791. Kentucky, until after Wayne's treaty, in 1795, was continually exposed to incursions from the Indians; yet, before Tom's day of manhood, the bloody contest between the white and the red men had terminated on the virgin soil of the new-born State—Kentucky was admitted into the Union in 1792. Yet the heroic struggles with the Indians by the early settlers were fresh in the memories of all. Prior to the settlement of Kentucky by white men, the Southern and Northwestern tribes of Indians were in the habit of hunting here as upon neutral ground. No wigwam had been erected, but it was claimed by all as a hunting ground. The frequent and fierce conflicts that occurred upon the meeting of the Indian tribes, together with conflicts with white men, caused the Indians first to call Kentucky "*The dark and bloody ground.*" At no point on the American Continent had the hatred between the two races risen to a higher point. Long after the peace between

England and America, and the close of the war of American Independence, the conflict between the white and red men in Kentucky was a war of extermination. The quiet cabin of the white man was frequently entered, under cover of night, by some roving band of Indians, and women and children tomahawked in cold blood. White men when taken by them, whether in the field at work, or behind a tree, watching their opportunity to shoot an Indian, were taken off to their towns in Ohio and burned at the stake, or tortured to death in a most cruel manner. No wonder the early settler in Kentucky swore eternal vengeance against the Indian who crossed his path, whether in peace or war. In a land where the white woman has cleaved the skull of the red warrior with an ax, who attempted to enter her cabin rifle in hand, from whence all but her had fled—who shall refuse to remember the heroines of the early settlers, and the historic name of the *dark and bloody ground*.

When Tom Fairfield arrived at manhood, the golden wing of peace was spread over the new-born State, from the Cumberland Mountains to the Ohio river.

A tract of land embracing a beautiful undulating surface, with a black and fertile soil, the forest growth of which is black walnut, cherry, honey locust, buckeye, pawpaw, sugar maple, elm, ash, hawthorn, coffee-tree and yellow poplar, entwined with grape vines of large size, which has been denominated the garden of Kentucky.

Many of the phrases, familiar to our grandfathers, have become obsolete, such as latch-string, bee-crossing, hunting-shirt, log-rolling, hominy-block, pack-horse and pack-saddle.

While many of their customs have been entirely forgotten, or never known, by the present generation, a history of some of the events of the time cannot fail to be interesting.

Tom had learned to read and write in Virginia, and this accomplishment frequently gave him employment, for many of the early settlers were glad to pay him for his assistance in this line of business, and it suited Tom to change his place of abode and character of employment. He was industrious, but never firm in his purpose, frequently commencing an enterprise, but always ready to abandon it in the middle.

Socially he was a great favorite at all wedding parties, and weddings were of frequent occurrence about this time.

For while Kentucky was over-run with Indians, the female portion of families were slow to immigrate to the scene of such bloody strife, and many of the early planters were young men, who found themselves bachelors for the want of female association. But with the influx of population now taking place, females largely predominated.

A wedding in Kentucky at that time was a day of rejoicing, and the young men in hearing distance all considered themselves invited. A fine dinner or supper was always prepared; of wine they had none, but distilling *corn whisky* was among the first industries of Kentucky, and at every wedding there was a custom called *running for the bottle*, which was of course a bottle of whisky.

The father of the bride, or some male acquaintance at the house of the bride — about one hour previous to the time announced for the ceremony — would stand on the door-step with the bottle in his hand, ready to deliver it to the first young man that approached him. At the appointed time the young men of the neighborhood would rendezvous at a point agreed upon, and when all were ready and the word *go* given, the race for the bottle, on fine horses, to the number of fifteen or twenty, was amusing and highly exciting. Tom had the good fortune to be the owner of a fleet horse—to own a fine horse and saddle was ever the pride and ambition of the young Kentuckian—and he won many bottles; but the end proved that it was bad instead of good luck, for Tom subsequently became too fond of the bottle.

Tom was young and hopeful, far away from his kindred, and he also married the daughter of an Englishman, who was not so fortunate as to be the owner of any portion of the virgin soil, but distinguished himself as a fine gardener, and all the inheritance Tom received with his wife was a *cart-load of gourds.*

You laugh, but you must remember that a few pewter plates and cob-handle knives was all that adorned the cupboards of some of our fathers, and gourds of different size made useful vessels. Coffee was not much in use, and in the dawn of the Revolution a party of brave Americans had thrown a ship-load of tea into the sea.

Tom, like many of the young planters, built a cabin upon a tract of land, under the Henderson claim, as purchased from the Cherokee Indians, which claim was subsequently set aside by the State of Virginia.

Tom, as we have said, was of a restless disposition, and from a planter he turned to be a boatman. Leaving his family at home in their cabin, he engaged to make a trip to Fort Washington (Cincinnati, then a village) on a keel-boat, descending the Kentucky and ascending the Ohio rivers. On this trip he first beheld the stupendous precipices on the Kentucky river, where the banks in many places are three hundred feet high, of solid limestone, and the beautiful country at he mouth of the Kentucky, on the Ohio river.

He was absent from home three months, for prior to steam navigation, the Ohio had been navigated by keel and flat-bottom boats for a quarter of a century, and many of the old boatmen were men of dissipated habits — *bad school for Tom.* When he returned home it was too late in the season to raise a crop. The next winter was long and cold. Tom and his little family keenly felt the grasp of poverty, and many times, in the dead hour of night, when the cold wind made the only audible sound on the outside, the latch-string of the cabin door had been pulled in, and the fire burned down to a bed of coals, Tom and his wife sat quietly and sadly by the dim light of a tallow candle, and told the stories of their families. Tom intended at some future time to return to Virginia and claim an inheritance, although, as he said, he was not the eldest son of his father, and by the laws of Virginia the eldest son is entitled to all of the estate in land, which, as he said, caused him to leave home; but from other sources he hoped in the future to reap the benefit of an inheritance.

Tom's wife, in her turn, told the story of her ancestors in the old country, and how she lived in hope of some revival of family fortune, which by the discovery of the necessary papers, would give her the means of rising above the cold grasp of poverty, so keenly felt by them; and many times through the long nights of winter, in that secret chamber where no intruder comes, Tom and his wife, whom he always called by the endearing name of *mother*, with a heart-felt desire to honor his infant children, had many long and interesting interviews upon the subject of the *ups* and *downs* of family fortune.

The joyous days of spring dawned upon the little household, and with it new ideas in the mind of Tom Fairfield; it was to become a *preacher;* why not? He could read—and must according to the philosophy of the people understand the Scriptures. Whatever may have been the delinquency of the early settlers in Kentucky, they were devotedly a religious people.

Ministers of the gospel were not required to study Theology; to be able to *read* was the only accomplishment, except the *call*; it was thought indispensable that a *preacher* should have *a divine call.*

Whatever may be said of ignorant worship, many of the early *preachers* in Kentucky were men of sterling piety, and did much to elevate and improve the rude society of the backwoodsmen. What they lacked in learning they made up in earnestness and a strict devotion to the *Master's cause;* what they lacked in eloquence they made up in force. Some extracts from the sermons of these old men have been preserved. I quote from one handed me by a friend:

"As Mo-ses lif-ted up the ser-pent in the wil-der-ness—ah! e-v-e-n so must the Son of M-a-n be lif-ted up—ah! That who so-e-v-e-r look up-on him—ah! m-a-y not p-e-r-i-s-h—ah! but h-a-ve e-v-e-r-l-a-sting l-i-f-e—ah!"

Notwithstanding this halting delivery, these old men laid the foundation of the refined and elegant society now enjoyed in Kentucky.

Tom Fairfield wished to improve his fortune and position in society—pay for preaching was small—but the many little needs of a family frequently fell to the lot of a preacher's wife. With this object in view, and waiting for the *call,* Tom and his wife attended all the meetings. *A wonderful phenomenon* occurred about this time, that upset all of Tom's calculations—it was called the *jerks*. It was principally confined to the females—but men sometimes were victims of it.

During the church service, and generally about the time the preacher's earnestness had warmed the congregation, the *jerks* would set in. Some one in the congregation would commence throwing the head and upper part of the body backward and forward, the motion would gradually increase, assuming a spasmodic appearance, until all discretion would leave the person attacked, and they would continue to *jerk* regardless of all modesty, until they *jerked* themselves upon the floor.

Tom and his wife one day attended the meeting of a *sect*, then called the "*New Lights.*" During the service Tom's wife was attacked with the *jerks*; the motion slow at first became very rapid, her combs flew among the congregation, and her long black hair cracked like a wagon whip. Tom was very much frightened, but with the assistance of some friends the poor woman was taken home, and soon became quiet. Tom never attended meeting again.

The old adage that *bad luck* never comes single-handed, was now setting in with Tom. Soon after this event, Tom returned from his labor one cold, wet evening. *Mother*, as he always called his wife, was very dull and stupid. Tom had attended to all the duties of the little household, pulled in the latch-string of the cabin door, covered the coals on the hearth with ashes—as the old people used to say, to keep the *seed* of fire.

In the morning when he awakened, his faithful wife, dear mother, as he called her, was by his side, *cold* and *dead*.

With three little daughters in the cabin and nothing else in the wide world, for the title to his land had been set aside. Disheartened with his misfortunes, Tom, with his little daughters, moved to the Ohio river.

Port William was the name given to the first settlement ever made at the mouth of the Kentucky river.

Seventy miles above Louisville the Kentucky mingles its water with the Ohio river, the land on the east side of the Kentucky and on the south side of the Ohio, narrows into a sharp point—the water is deep up to the shore. When navigation first commenced this point was the keel-boat landing, and subsequently the steamboat landing.

Here, Dave Deminish kept a saloon, (then called a grocery). One room sixteen feet square, filled with *cheap John merchandise*, the principal article for sale was *corn whisky*, distilled in the upper counties, and shipped to Port William on keel boats,—this article was afterwards called *old Bourbon*.

Port William was blessed with the O!-be-joyful. Red-head Sam Sims run a whisky shop in connection with his tavern, but the point, or landing was the great place of attraction, here idle boatmen were always ready to entertain idle citizens. Old Brother Demitt owned large tracts of land, and a number of slaves, and of course he was a leader in society, why not? he was a member of the church if he did-stand on the street corners, tell low anecdotes, and drink whisky all-day-long. And old Arch Wheataker owned slaves to work for him, and he, of course, could ride his old ball-face sorrel horse to Port William, drink whisky all day and run old Ball home at night. Late in December one dark night, the Angel of observation was looking into the room of Dave Deminish. A tall man with silver gray hair was pleading with Dave for one more dram. They stood by the counter alone, and it was late, the customers had all gone save Tom Fairfield. Tom offered to pledge his coat as a guarantee for payment, Dave was anxious to close the store (as he called it), and he said mildly as he laid his hand softly on Tom's shoulder, "Keep your coat on, Tom," and handing him a glass of spoiled beer, affected friendship. In attempting to drink the beer Tom *heaved*. Dave was insulted, and kicked him out, and closed the door. On reeling feet, alone, and in the dark, Tom departed. In the middle of the night commenced a wonderful snow storm, and the dawn of morning found the earth covered with a white mantle twenty-four inches deep.

The ever diligent eye of the Angel of observation was peering into the cabin of Tom Fairfield, two miles distant from the *Point*, and one mile north of Brother Demitts. Roxie, the eldest daughter, found a few sticks of wood, which happened to be in doors, made up a little fire and was cooking some corn cakes. Rose had covered Suza with a tattered blanket, and was rocking her in a trough. The cold wind upon the outside carried away the inaudible murmurs of the little sisters.

At one o'clock in the evening the little fire had burned

out. Rose was still engaged with the baby, and Roxie passed the time between childish conversations with Rose about the deep snow, and their absent father, who she said would get the snow out of his way and come home after a while, then peeping out the crack of the door to watch for some one passing. Old Father Tearful had passed the cabin, his face and head wrapped up with a strap of sheepskin to ward off the cold, and he did not hear the cries of Roxie Fairfield. One hour later Suza was crying piteously and shivering with the cold.

Roxie said firmly to Rose, you pet and coax the poor thing and I will go to Aunt Katy's and get some one to come and, and get us some wood, making a great effort to conceal a half suppressed sob, and a starting tear. Then patting Rose on the head with her little hand said coaxingly, "Be good to-to-the baby, and I'll soon be back." Leaving both little sisters in tears, and pulling her little bonnet close 'round her ears, she left the cabin, and struggled bravely through the deep snow; fortunately when she gained the track of Father Tearful's horse she had less difficulty. The old man was riding a Conestoga horse whose feet and legs, from their large size, made quite an opening in the snow.

The Angel eye of observation peering into the east room of Brother Demitt's house, (he lived in a double cabin of hewn logs,) saw Aunt Katy sittting on one corner of the hearth-stone, busily plying her fingers upon a half finished stocking; upon the other corner lay a large dog; stretched at full length; half way between the two sat the old house-cat, eying the mastiff and the mistress, and ready to retreat from the first invader. The hickory logs in the fire-place were wrapping each other with the red flames of heat, and the cold wind rushing 'round the corner of the house was the only sound that disturbed the stillness of the hour.

With a sudden push the door swung upon its hinges,

and Roxie Fairfield, shivering with the cold, appeared upon the stage. Aunt Katy threw her head back, and looking under her specs, straight down her nose at the little intruder, said, in a voice half mingled with astonishment, "Roxie Fairfield, where in the name of heaven did you come from?" Roxie, nothing abashed by the question, replied in a plaintive tone, "Daddy didn't come home all night nor all day—and—and we're 'fraid the baby'll freeze." The simple narrative of the child told Aunt Katy the *whole story*. She knew Tom Fairfield, and although a drunkard, he would not thus desert his children. "Come to the fire, child," said Aunt Katy in a milder tone, and as she turned to the back door she said, mentally, "*dead, and covered with snow.*" She continued, "Joe, I say, Joe, get old Ned and hitch him to the wood slide, and go after the Fairfield children—*quick*—call Dick to help hitch up." Dick was an old negro who had the gout so bad in his left foot that he could not wear a shoe, and that foot wrapped up in a saddle blanket, made an impression in the snow about the size of an elephant's track.

Roxie made a start to return as she came, and while Aunt Katy was coaxing and persuading her to wait for the slide, Joe, a colored boy, and old Ned were gotten ready for the venture. Dick, by Aunt Katy's directions, had thrown a straw bed upon the slide, and bearing his weight upon his right foot, he caught Roxie by the arms and carefully placed her upon it.

Joe, as he held the rope-reins in one hand and a long switch in the other, turned his eyes upon the face of the little heroine, all mingled with doubt and fear, saying in a harsh tone, "keep yourself in the middle of the slide, puss, for I'm gwine to drive like litenin'."

Aunt Katy stood in the cold door gazing at the running horse and slide until they were out of sight, and then turning to Dick who, standing by the chimney, was holding his left foot close to the coals, said, "Tom Fairfield is dead and under the snow, poor soul! and them children will have to be *raised*, and I'll bet the nittin' of five pair of stockins that old Demitt will try to poke one of 'em on me."

Joe soon returned with the precious charge. He had Suza, the baby, in her rocking trough, well wrapped up in the old blanket and placed in the middle of the slide, with Roxie seated on one side and Rose on the other. The slide had no shafts by which the old horse could hold it back; it was Dick's office to hold back with a rope when drawing wood, but he was too slow for this trip, and Joe's long switch served to keep old Ned ahead of the slide when traveling down hill.

A large fire and a warm room, with Aunt Katy's pacifying tones of voice, soon made the little sisters comparatively happy; she promised them that daddy would soon return.

The news soon spread through the neighborhood, and every one who knew Tom Fairfield solemnly testified that he would not desert his children; the irresistible conclusion was that while intoxicated he was frozen, and that he lay dead under the snow.

A council of the settlers, (for all were considered neighbors for ten miles 'round,) was called, over which Brother Demitt presided. Aunt Katy, as the nearest neighbor and first benefactress, claimed the pre-emption right to the first choice, which was of course granted. Roxie, the eldest, was large enough to perform some service in a family, and Rose would soon be; Suza, the baby, was the trouble. Aunt Katy was called upon to take her choice before other preliminaries could be settled.

Suza, the baby, with her bright little eyes, red cheeks and proud efforts, to stand alone, had won Aunt Katy's affections, and she, without any persuasion on the part of old Demitt, emphatically declared that Suza should never leave her house until she left it as a free woman.

Mrs. Evaline Estep and Aunt Fillis Foster were the contending candidates for Rose and Roxie.

Brother Demitt decided that Aunt Fillis should take Roxie, and Mrs. Estep should be foster mother to Rose, with all the effects left in the Fairfield cabin.

These ladies lived four miles from the Demitt house, in different directions. With much persuasion and kind treatment they bundled up the precious little charges and departed.

While the Angel of sorrow hovered 'round the little hearts of the deparated sisters.

SCENE FOURTH—ROXIE DAYMON AND ROSE SIMON.

>The road of life is light and dark,
>Each journeyman will make his mark;
>The mark is seen by all behind,
>Excepting those who go stark blind.
>Men for women mark out the way,
>In spite of all the rib can say;
>But when the way is rough and hard,
>The woman's eye will come to guard
>The footsteps of her liege and lord,
>With gentle tone and loving word.

Since the curtain fell upon the closing sentence in the last scene, many long and tedious seasons have passed away.

The placid waters of the beautiful Ohio have long since been disturbed by steam navigation; and the music of the steam engine echoing from the river hills have alarmed the bat and the owl, and broke the solitude around the graves of many of the first settlers. Many old associations have lived and died. The infant images of the early settlers are men and women. In the order of time Roxie Fairfield, the heroine of the snow storm, and Aunt Fillis Foster, claim our attention.

With a few back glances at girlhood, we hasten on to her womanhood. Aunt Fillis permitted Roxie to attend a country school a few months in each year. The school house was built of round logs, was twenty feet square, with one log left out on the south side for a window. The seats were made of slabs from the drift wood on the Ohio River, (the first cut from the log, one side flat, the other having the shape of the log, rounding); holes were bored in the slabs and pins eighteen inches long inserted for legs. These benches were set against the wall of the room, and the pupils arranged sitting in rows around the room. In the center sat the teacher by a little square table, with a switch long enough to reach any pupil in the house without rising from his seat. And thus the heroine of the snow storm received the rudiments of an education, as she grew to womanhood.

Roxie was obedient, tidy—and twenty, and like all girls of her class, had a lover. Aunt Fillis said Roxie kept everything about the house in the right place, and was always in the right place herself; she said more, she could not keep house without her. By what spirit Aunt Fillis was animated we shall not undertake to say, but she forbade Roxie's lover the prerogative of her premises.

Roxie's family blood could never submit to slavery, and she ran away with her lover, was married according to the common law, which recognizes man and wife as one, and the man is that one.

They went to Louisville, and the reader has already been introduced to the womanhood of Roxie Fairfield in the person of Daymon's wife.

The reader is referred to the closing sentence of Scene First. Daymon was granted a new trial, which never came off, and the young couple left Louisville and went to Chicago, Illinois. Roxie had been concealed by a female friend, and only learned the fate of Daymon a few minutes before she entered the court room. Daymon resolved to reform, for when future hope departed, and all but life had fled, the faithful Roxie rose like a spirit from the dead to come and stand by him.

Daymon and Roxie left Louisville without any intimation of their destination to any one, without anything to pay expenses, and nothing but their wearing apparel, both resolved to work, for the sun shone as brightly upon them as it did upon any man and woman in the world.

As a day laborer Daymon worked in and around the infant city, as ignorant of the bright future as the wild ducks that hovered 'round the shores of the lake.

It is said that P. J. Marquette, a French missionary from Canada, was the first white man that settled on the spot where Chicago now stands. This was before the war of the Revolution, and his residence was temporary.

Many years afterward a negro from San Domingo made some improvements at the same place; but John Kinzie is generally regarded as the first settler at Chicago, for he made a permanent home there in 1804. For a quarter of a century the village had less than one hundred inhabitants. A wild onion that grew there, called by the Indians Chikago, gave the name to the city.

After a few years of hard labor and strict economy, a land-holder was indebted to Daymon the sum of one hundred and fifty dollars. Daymon wished to collect his dues and emigrate farther west. By the persuasion of Roxie he was induced to accept a deed to fifteen acres of land. In a short time he sold one acre for more than the cost of the whole tract, and was soon selling by the foot instead of the acre. The unparalleled growth of the city made Daymon rich in spite of himself.

The ever wakeful eye of the Angel of observation is peering into the parlor of the Daymon *palace*, to see Roxie surrounded with all the luxuries of furniture, sitting by an ornamented table, upon which lay gilt-edged paper; in the center of the table sat a pearl ink-stand and a glass ornament set with variegated colors. Roxie's forehead rested upon the palm of her left hand, elbow on the table. Profound reflections are passing through her brain; they carry her back to the days of her childhood. Oh, how she loved Suza; the little bright eyes gazed upon her and the red lips pronounced the inaudible sound, *"dear sister."* "Yes, I will write," said Roxie, mentally. She takes the gold pen in her right hand, adjusting the paper with her left, she *paused* to thank from the bottom of her heart old Ben Robertson, who in the country school had taught her the art of penmanship. *Hush!* did the hall bell ring? In a few minutes a servant appeared at the door and announced the name of Aunt Patsy Perkins.

"Admit Aunt Patsy — tell her your mistress is at home," said Roxie, rising from the table.

Aunt Patsy Perkins was floating upon the surface of upper-tendom in Chicago. She understood all of the late styles; a queen in the drawing-room, understood the art precisely of entertaining company; the grandest ladies in the city would listen to the council of Aunt Patsy, for she could talk faster and more of it than any woman west of the Alleghany Mountains.

The visitor enters the room; Roxie offers Aunt Patsy an easy chair; Aunt Patsy is wiping away the perspiration with a fancy kerchief, in one hand, and using the fan with the other. When seated she said:

"I must rest a little, for I have something to tell you, and I will tell you now what it is before I begin. Old Perkins has no more love for style than I have for his *dratted poor kin.* But as I was going to tell you, Perkins received a letter from Indiana, stating this Cousin Sally wished to make us a visit. She's a plain, poor girl, that knows no more of style than Perkins does of a woman's comforts. I'll tell you what it is, Mrs. Daymon, if she does come, if I don't make it hot for old Perkins, it'll be because I can't talk. A woman has nothing but her tongue, and while I live I will use mine."

Then pointing her index finger at Roxie, continued: "I will tell you what it is Mrs. Daymon, take two white beans out of one hull, and place them on the top of the garden fence, and then look at 'em across the garden, and if you can tell which one is the largest, you can seen what difference there is in the way old Perkins hates style and I hate his *dratted poor kin*. What wealthy families are to do in this city, God only knows. I think sometimes old Perkins is a *wooden man*, for, with all my style, I can make no more impression on h-i-m, than I can upon an oak stump, Mrs. Daymon. What if he did make a thousand dollars last week, when he wants to stick his *poor kin* 'round me, like stumps in a flower garden."

At this point Roxie ventured to say a word. "Aunt Patsy, I thought Jim was kinsfolk on your side of the house."

"Yes, but honey, I am good to Jim, poor soul, he knows it," said Aunt Patsy gravely, and then she paused.

Jim was a poor boy, eighteen years old, and the son of Aunt Patsy's dear brother, long since laid under the dark green sod of Indiana. The poor boy, hearing of the wealth of his Aunt Patsy, had come to Chicago and was working on the streets, poorly clad.

Aunt Patsy would sometimes give him a few dollars, as you would throw a bone to a dog, requesting him at the same time to always come to the back door, and never be about the house when she had company.

Aunt Patsy said emphatically, as she left the Daymon palace, "I'll tell you what it is, Mrs. Daymon, I'm goin' home to study human nature, and if I don't find some avenue to reach old Perkins, I shall take the liberty to insult the first one of his *dratted poor kin* that sets foot in my house."

After Aunt Patsy left, Roxie thought no more of her letter of inquiry, and company engaged her attention for some days until the subject passed entirely out of her mind.

Soon after these events Roxie died with the cholera—

leaving an only daughter—and was buried as ignorant of the fate of her sister as the stone that now stands upon her grave.

We must now turn back more than a decade, which brings us to the burning of the steamboat Brandywine, on the Mississippi river. The boat was heavily freighted, with a large number of passengers on board; the origin of the fire has never been positively known; it was late in the night, with a heavy breeze striking the boat aft, where the fire occurred. In a short time all on board was in confusion; the pilot, from the confusion of the moment, or the lack of a proper knowledge of the river, headed the boat for the wrong shore, and she ran a-ground on a deep sand bar a long way from shore and burned to the waters' edge; between the two great elements of fire and water many leaped into the river and were drowned, and some reached the shore on pieces of the wreck. Among those fortunate enough to reach the shore was an Englishman, who was so badly injured he was unable to walk; by the more fortunate he was carried to the cabin of a wood cutter, where he soon after died.

When he fully realized the situation he called for ink and paper; there was none on the premises; a messenger was dispatched to the nearest point where it was supposed the articles could be obtained, but he was too late. When the last moments came the dying man made the following statement: "My name is John A. Lasco. I have traveled for three years in this country without finding the slightest trace of the object of my search—an only and a dear sister. Her name is Susan Lasco; with our father she left the old country many years ago. They were poor,—the family fortune being held in abeyance by the loss of some papers. I remained, but our father gave up all hope and emigrated to America, taking Susan with him. In the course of nature the old man is dead, and my sister Susan, if she is living, is the last, or soon will be the last, link of the family. I am making this statement as my last will and testament. Some years ago the post-master in my native town received a letter from America stating that by the confession of one, Alonzo Phelps, who was condemned to die, that there was a bundle of papers concealed in a certain place by him before he left the country. Search was made and the papers found which gave me the possession of the family estate. The letter was subscribed D. C., which gave a poor knowledge of the writer. I sold the property and emigrated to this country in search of my sister; I have had poor success. She probably married, and the ceremony changed her name, and I fear she is hopelessly lost to her rights; her name was Susan Lasco—what it is now, God only knows. But to Susan Lasco, and her descendants, I will the sum of twenty thousand dollars, now on deposit in a western bank; the certificate of deposit names the bank; the papers are wet and now upon my person; the money in my pocket, $110, I will to the good woman of this house—with a request that she will carefully dry and preserve my papers, and deliver them to some respectable lawyer in Memphis—at this point the speaker was breathing hard—his tone of voice almost inaudible. At his request, made by signs, he was turned over and died in a few moments without any further directions.

The inmates of the cabin, besides the good woman of the house, were only a few wood cutters, among whom stood Brindle Bill, of Shirt-Tail Bend notoriety. Bill, to use his own language, was *strap'd*, and was chopping wood at this point to raise a little money upon which to make another start. Many years had passed away since he left Shirt Tail Bend. He had been three times set on shore, from steamboats, for playing sharp tricks at three card monte upon passengers, and he had gone to work, which he never did until he was entirely out of money. Brindle Bill left the cabin, *ostensibly* to go to work; but he sat upon the log, rubbed his hand across his forehead, and said mentally, "Su-san La-s-co. By the last card in the deck, *that is the name;* if I didn't hear Simon's wife, in Shirt-Tail Bend, years ago, say her mother's name was S-u-s-a-n L-a-s-c-o. I will never play another game; and—and *twenty thousand in bank.* By hell, I've struck a lead."

The ever open ear of the Angel of observation was catching the sound of a conversation in the cabin of Sundown Hill in Shirt-Tail Bend. It was as follows—

"Many changes, Bill, since you left here; the Carlo wood yard has play'd out; Don Carlo went back to Kentucky. I heard he was blowed up on a steamboat; if he ever come down again I did'nt hear of it."

"Hope he never did," said Bill, chawing the old grudge with his eye teeth.

Hill continued: "You see, Bill, the old wood yards have given place to plantations. Simon, your old friend, is making pretentions to be called a planter," said Sundown Hill to Brindle Bill, in a tone of confidence.

"Go slow, Hill, there is a hen on the nest. I come back here to play a strong game; twenty thousand in bank," and Brindle Bill winked with his right eye, the language of which is, I deal and you play the cards I give you. "You heard of the burning of the Brandywine; well, there was an Englishman went up in that scrape, and he left twenty thousand in bank, and Rose Simon is the *heir,*" said Bill in a tone of confidence.

"And what can that profit y-o-u?" said Hill rather indignantly.

"I am playing this game; I want you to send for Simon," said Bill rather commandingly.

"Simon has changed considerably since you saw him; and, besides, fortunes that come across the water seldom prove true. Men who have fortunes in their native land seldom seek fortunes in a strange country," said Hill argumentatively.

"There is no mistake in this case, for uncle John had the *di-dapper eggs* in his pocket," said Bill firmly.

Late that evening three men, in close council, were seen in Shirt-Tail Bend. S. S. Simon had joined the company of the other two. After Brindle Bill had related to Simon the events above described, the following questions and answers passed between the two:

"Mrs. Simon's mother was named Susan Lasco?"

"Undoubtedly; and her father's name was Tom Fairfield. She is the brave woman who broke up, or rather burned up, the gambling den in Shirt-Tail Bend. We were married in Tennessee. Mrs. Simon was the adopted daughter of Mrs. Evaline Estep, her parents having died when she was quite young. The old lady Estep tried to horn me off; but I *beat her*. Well the old christian woman gave Rose a good many things, among which was a box of family keepsakes; she said they were given to her in consideration of her taking the youngest child of the orphan children. There may be something in that box to identify the family."

At this point Brindle Bill winked his right eye—it is my deal, you play the cards I give you. As Simon was about to leave the company, to break the news to his wife, Brindle Bill said to him very confidentially: "You find out in what part of the country this division of the orphan children took place, and whenever you find that place, be where it will, right there is where I was raised—the balance of them children is *dead*, Simon," and he again winked his right eye.

"I understand," said Simon, and as he walked on towards home to apprise Rose of her good fortune, he said mentally, "This is Bill's deal, I will play the cards he gives me." Simon was a shifty man; he stood in the *half-way house* between the honest man and the rogue; was always ready to take anything he could lay hands on, as long as he could hold some one else between himself and danger. Rose Simon received the news with delight. She hastened to her box of keepsakes and held before Simon's astonished eyes an old breast-pin with this inscription: "Presented to Susan Lasco by her brother, John A. Lasco, 1751." "That's all the evidence we want," said Simon emphatically. "Now," continued Simon, coaxingly, "What became of your sisters?"

"You know when Mrs. Estep moved to Tennessee I was quite small. I have heard nothing of my sisters since that time. It has been more than fifteen years," said Rose gravely.

"At what point in Kentucky were you separated?" said Simon inquiringly.

"Port William, the mouth of the Kentucky river," said Rose plainly.

"Brindle Bill says they are dead," said Simon slowly.

"B-r-i-n-d-l e B-i-l-l, why, I would not believe him on oath," said Rose indignantly.

"Yes, but he can prove it," said Simon triumphantly, and he then continued, "If we leave any gaps down, *my dear*, we will not be able to draw the money until those sisters are hunted up, and then it would cut us down to less than seven thousand dollars—and that would hardly build us a fine house," and with many fair and coaxing words Simon obtained a promise from Rose that she would permit him to manage the business.

At the counter of a western bank stood S. S. Simon and party presenting the certificate of deposit for twenty thousand dollars. In addition to the breast-pin Rose had unfolded an old paper, that had laid for years in the bottom of her box. It was a certificate of the marriage of Tom Fairfield and Susan Lasco. Brindle Bill and Sundown Hill were sworn and testified that Rose Simon *alias* Rose Fairfield was the only surviving child of Tom Fairfield and Susan Lasco. Brindle Bill said he was raised in Port William, and was at the funeral of the little innocent years before. The money was paid over. Rose did not believe a word that Bill said but she had promised Simon that she would let him manage the business, and few people will refuse money when it is thrust upon them.

The party returned to Shirt-Tail Bend. Simon deceived Rose with the plea of some little debts, paid over to Brindle Bill and Sundown Hill three hundred dollars each. Brindle Bill soon got away with three hundred dollars; "*Strop'd* again," he said mentally, and then continued, "Some call it blackmailin' or backmailin', but I call it a *back-handed* game. It is nothing but making use of power, and if a fellow don't use power when it's put in his hands he had better bunch tools and quit.

Brindle Bill said to S. S. Simon, "I have had a streak of bad luck; lost all my money; want to borrow three hundred dollars. No use to say you havn't got it, for I can find them sisters of your wife in less than three weeks," and he winked his right eye.

Simon hesitated, but finally with many words of caution paid over the money.

Soon after these events S. S. Simon was greatly relieved by reading in a newspaper the account of the sentence of Brindle Bill to the state prison for a long term of years.

S. S. Simon now stood in the front rank of the planters of his neighborhood; had built a new house and ready to furnish it; Rose was persuaded by him to make the trip with him to New Orleans and select her furniture for the new house. While in the city Rose Simon was attacked with the yellow fever and died on the way home. She was buried in Louisiana, intestate and childless.

SCENE FIFTH.—THE BELLE OF PORT WILLIAM.

> A cozy room, adorned with maiden art,
> Contained the belle of Port William's heart.
> There she stood—to blushing love unknown,
> Her youthful heart was all her own.
> Her sisters gone, and every kindred tie,
> Alone she smiled, alone she had to cry;
> No mother's smile, no father's kind reproof,
> She hop'd and pray'd beneath a stranger's roof.

The voice of history and the practice of historians has been to dwell upon the marching of armies; the deeds of great heroes; the rise and fall of governments; great battles and victories; the conduct of troops, etc., while the manners and customs of the people of whom they write are entirely ignored.

Were it not for the common law of England, we would have a poor knowledge of the manners and customs of the English people long centuries ago.

The common law was founded upon the manners and customs of the people, and many of the principles of the common law have come down to the present day. And a careful study of the common laws of England is the best guide to English civilization long centuries ago.

Manners and customs change with almost every generation, yet the principles upon which our manners and customs are founded are less changeable.

Change is marked upon almost everything It is said

that the particles which compose our bodies change in every seven years. The oceans and continents change in a long series of ages. Change is one of the universal laws of matter.

And like everything else, Port William changed. Brother Demitt left Port William, on foot and full of whisky, one cold evening in December. The path led him across a field fenced from the suburbs of the village. The old man being unable to mount the fence, sat down to rest with his back against the fence—here it is supposed he fell into a stupid sleep. The cold north wind—that never ceases to blow because some of Earth's poor children are intoxicated—wafted away the spirit of the old man, and his neighbors, the next morning, found the old man sitting against the fence, frozen, cold and dead.

Old Arch Wheataker, full of whisky, was running old Ball for home one evening in the twilight. Old Ball, frightened at something by the side of the road, threw the old man against a tree, and "busted" his head.

Dave Deminish had retired from business and given place to the brilliantly lighted saloon. Old Dick, the negro man, was sleeping beneath the sod, with as little pain in his left foot as any other member of his body. Joe, the colored boy that drove the wood slide so fast through the snow with the little orphan girls, had left home, found his way to Canada, and was enjoying his freedom in the Queen's Dominion.

The Demitt estate had passed through the hands of administrators much reduced. Old Demitt died intestate, and Aunt Katy had no children. His relations inherited his estate, except Aunt Katy's life interest. But Aunt Katy had money of her own, earned with her own hands.

Aunt Katy was economical and industrious. Every dry goods store in Port William was furnished with stockings knit by the hands of Aunt Katy. The passion to save in Aunt Katy's breast, like Aaron's serpent, swallowed up the rest.

Aunt Katy was a good talker—except of her own concerns, upon which she was non-committal. She kept her own counsel and her own money. It was supposed by the Demitt kinsfolk that Aunt Katy had a will filed away, and old Ballard, the administrator, was often interrogated by the Demitt kinsfolk about Aunt Katy's will. Old Ballard was a cold man of business—one that never thought of anything that did not pay him—and, of course, sent all will-hunters to Aunt Katy.

The Demitt relations indulged in many speculations about Aunt Katy's money. Some counted it by the thousand, and all hoped to receive their portion when the poor old woman slept beneath the sod.

Aunt Katy had moved to Port William, to occupy one of the best houses in the village, in which she held a life estate. Aunt Katy's household consisted of herself and Suza Fairfield, eleven years old, and it was supposed by the Demitt relations, that when Aunt Katy died, a will would turn up in favor of Suza Fairfield.

Tom Ditamus had moved from the backwoods of the Cumberland mountains to the Ohio river, and not pleased with the surroundings of his adopted locality, made up his mind to return to his old home. Tom had a wife and two dirty children. Tom's wife was a pussy-cat woman, and obeyed all of Tom's commands without ever stopping to think on the subject of "woman's rights." Tom was a sulky fellow; his forehead retreated from his eyebrows, at an angle of forty-five degrees, to the top of his head; his skull had a greater distance between the ears than it had fore and aft'; a dark shade hung in the corner of his eye, and he stood six feet above the dirt with square shoulders. Tom was too great a coward to steal, and too lazy to work. Tom intended to return to his old home in a covered wagon drawn by an ox team.

The Demitt relations held a council, and appointed one of their number to confer with Tom Ditamus and engage him to take Suza Fairfield—with his family and in his wagon—to the backwoods of the Cumberland Mountains. For, they said, thus spirited away Aunt Katy would never hear from her; and Aunt Katy's money, when broken loose from where she was damming it up, by the death of the old thing would flow in its legitimate channel.

And the hard-favored and the hard-hearted Tom agreed to perform the job for ten dollars.

It was in the fall of the year and a foggy morning. When the atmosphere is heavy the cold of the night produces a mist by condensing the dampness of the river, called fog; it is sometimes so thick, early in the morning, that the eye cannot penetrate it more than one hundred yards.

Tom was ready to start, and fortunately for him, seeing Suza Fairfield passing his camp, he approached her. She thought he wished to make some inquiry, and stood still until the strong man caught her by the arm, with one hand in the other hand he held an ugly gag, and told her if she made any noise he would put the bit in her mouth and tie the straps on the back of her head. The child made one scream, but as Tom prepared to gag her she submitted, and Tom placed her in his covered wagon between his dirty children, giving the gag to his wife, and commanding her if Suza made the slightest noise to put the bridle on her, and in the dense clouds of fog Tom drove his wagon south.

Suza realized that she was captured, but for what purpose she could not divine; with a brave heart—far above her years—she determined to make her escape the first night, for after that she said, mentally, she would be unable to find home. She sat quietly and passed the day in reflection, and resolved in her mind that she would leave the caravan of Tom Ditamus that night, or die in the attempt. She remembered the words of Aunt Katy—"Discretion is the better part of valor"—and upon that theory the little orphan formed her plan.

The team traveled slow, for Tom was compelled to let them rest—in the warm part of the day—the sun at last disappeared behind the western horizon. To the unspeakable delight of the little prisoner, in a dark wood by the shore of a creek, Tom encamped for the night, building a fire by the side of a large log. The party in the wagon, excepting Suza, were permitted to come out and sit by the fire. While Tom's wife was preparing supper, Suza imploringly begged Tom to let her come to the fire, for she had something to tell him. Tom at last consented, but said cautiously, "you must talk low." "*Oh! I will talk so easy*," said Suza, in a stage whisper. She was permitted to take her seat with the party on a small log, and here for an hour she entertained them with stories of abuse that she had received from the *old witch, Aunt Katy*, and emphatically declared that she would go anywhere to get away from the *old witch*.

The orphan girl, eleven years of age, threw Tom Ditamus, a man thirty-five years of age, entirely off his guard. Tom thought he had a *soft thing* and the whole party were soon sound asleep, except Suza.

With a step as light as a timid cat, Suza Fairfield left Tom Ditamus and his family sleeping soundly on the bank of the creek in the dark woods, and sped toward Port William. They had traveled only ten miles with a lazy ox team and the active feet of the little captive could soon retrace the distance, if she did not lose the way; to make assurance doubly sure, Suza determined to follow the Kentucky river, for she knew that would take her to Port William; the road was part of the way on the bank of the river, but sometimes diverged into the hills a considerable distance from the river. At those places Suza would follow the river, though her path was through dense woods and in places thickly set with underbrush and briars. Onward the brave little girl would struggle, until again relieved by the friendly road making its appearance again upon the bank of the river, and then the nimble little feet would travel at the rate of four miles an hour. Again Suza would have to take to the dark woods, with no lamp to guide her footsteps but the twinkling distant star. In one of these ventures Suza was brought to a stand, by the mouth of White's creek pouring its lazy waters into the Kentucky river. The water was deep and dark. Suza stood and reflected. An owl broke the stillness of the night on the opposite side of the creek. The last note of his voice seemed to say, *come over—over—little gal.* Suza sank upon the ground and wept bitterly. It is said that the cry of a goose once saved Rome. The seemingly taunting cry of the owl did not save Suza, but her own good sense taught her that she could trace the creek on the south side until she would find a ford, and when across the creek retrace it back on the north side to the unerring river; and although this unexpected fate had perhaps doubled her task, she had resolved to perform it. She remembered Aunt Katy's words, "if there is a will, there is a way," and onward she sped for two long hours. Suza followed the zigzag course of the bewildering creek, and found herself at last in the big road stretching up from the water of the creek. She recognized the ford, for here she had passed in the hateful prison wagon, and remembered that the water was not more than one foot deep. Suza pulled off her little shoes and waded the creek; when upon the north side she looked at the dark woods, on the north bank of the creek, and at the friendly road, so open and smooth to her little feet, and said, mentally, "this road will lead me to Port William, and I will follow it, if Tom Ditamus does catch me;" and onward she sped.

The dawn of morning had illuminated the eastern sky,

when Suza Fairfield beheld the broad and beautiful bottom land of the Ohio river.

No mariner that ever circumnavigated the globe could have beheld his starting point with more delight than Suza Fairfield beheld the chimneys in Port William. She was soon upon the home street, and saw the chimney of Aunt Katy's house; no smoke was rising from it as from others; everything about the premises was as still as the breath of life on the Dead Sea. Suza approached the back yard, the door of Aunt Katy's room was not fastened, it turned upon its hinges as Suza touched it; Aunt Katy's bed was not tumbled; the fire had burned down; in front of the smoldering coals Aunt Katy sat upon her easy chair, her face buried in her hands, elbows upon her knees—Suza paused—*Aunt Katy sleeps;* a moment's reflection, and then Suza laid her tiny hand upon the gray head of the sleeping woman, and pronounced the words, nearest her little heart in a soft, mellow tone, "A-u-n-t K-a-t-y."

In an instant Aunt Katy Demitt was pressing Suza Fairfield close to her old faithful heart.

Old and young tears were mingled together for a few minutes, and then Suza related her capture and escape as we have recorded it; at the close of which Suza was nearly out of breath. Aunt Katy threw herself upon her knees by the bedside and covered her face with the palms of her hands. Suza reflected, and thought of something she had not related, and starting toward the old mother with the words on her tongue when the Angel of observation placed his finger on her lips, with the audible sound of *hush!* Aunt Katy's praying.

Aunt Katy rose from her posture with the words: "I understand it all my child; the Demitts want you out of the way. Well, if they get the few four pences that I am able to scrape together old Katy Demitt will give 'em the last sock that she ever expects to knit; forewarned, fore-armed, my child. As for Tom Ditamus, he may go for what he is worth. He has some of the Demitt money, no doubt, and I have a warning that will last me to the grave. Old Demitt had one fault, but God knows his kinsfolk have thousands."

Aunt Katy took Suza by the hand and led her to the hiding place, and Suza Fairfield, for the first time, beheld Aunt Katy's money—five hundred dollars in gold and silver—and the old foster mother's will, bequeathing all her earthly possessions to Suza Fairfield. The will was witnessed by old Ballard and old Father Tearful. And from thence forward Suza was the only person in the wide world in full possession of Aunt Katy Demitt's secrets. Tantalized by her relations, Aunt Katy was like a student of botany, confined in the center of a large plain with a single flower, for she doated on Suza Fairfield with a love seldom realized by a foster mother.

Tom Ditamus awoke the next morning (perhaps about the time Suza entered Port William) and found the little prisoner gone. Tom did not care; he had his money, and he yoked up his cattle and traveled on.

We must now look forward more than a decade in order to speak of Don Carlo, the hero of Shirt-Tail Bend, whom, in our haste to speak of other parties, we left at the half-way castle in a senseless condition, on the fatal day of the explosion of the Red Stone.

The half-way castle was one of the first brick houses ever built on the Ohio river. It had long been the property of infant heirs, and rented out or left unoccupied; it stood on the southern bank of the river about half way between Louisville and Cincinnati, hence the name of the half-way castle. Don Carlo was severely stunned, but not fatally injured; he had sold out in Shirt-Tail Bend, and was returning to the home of his childhood when the dreadful accident occured. Don had saved a little sum of money with which he had purchased a small farm in Kentucky, and began to reflect that he was a bachelor. Numerous friends had often reminded him that a brave young lady had rushed into the water and dragged his lifeless body to the friendly shore, when in a few minutes more he would have been lost forever

Twelve months or more after these events a camp meeting was announced to come off in the neighborhood of Port William. Camp meetings frequently occurred at that day in Kentucky. The members of the church, or at least a large portion of them, would prepare to camp out and hold a protracted meeting. When the time and place were selected some of the interested parties would visit the nearest saw mill and borrow several wagon loads of lumber, draw it to the place selected, which was always in the woods near some stream or fountain of water, with the plank placed upon logs or stumps, they would erect the stand or pulpit, around the same, on three sides at most, they would arrange planks for seats by placing them upon logs and stumps; they would also build shanties and partly fill them with straw, upon which the campers slept. Fires were kindled outside for cooking purposes. Here they would preach and pray, hold prayer meetings and love feasts night and day, sometimes for two or three weeks. On the Sabbath day the whole country, old and young, for ten miles around, would attend the camp meeting.

Don Carlo said to a friend: "I shall attend the camp meeting, for I have entertained a secret desire for a long time to make the acquaintance of the young lady who it is said saved my life from the wreck of the Red Stone."

The camp meeting will afford the opportunity. It was on a Sabbath morning. Don and his friend were standing upon the camp ground; the people were pouring in from all directions; two young ladies passed them on their way to the stand; one of them attracted Don Carlo's attention, she was not a blonde nor a brunette, but half way between the two, inheriting the beauty of each. Don said to his friend; "There goes the prettiest woman in America."

Then rubbing his hand over his forehead, continued; "You are acquainted with people here, I wish you would make some inquiry of that lady's name and family."

"I thought you was hunting the girl that pulled you out of the river," said his friend, sarcastically.

"Yes, but I want to know the lady that has just passed us," said Don, gravely.

Love at first sight. Ah! what is love? It has puzzled mental philosophers of all ages; and no one has ever told us why a man will love one woman above all the balance of God's creatures. And then, the strangest secret in the problem is, that a third party can see nothing lovable in the woman so adored by her lord.

No wonder, the ancient Greeks represented cupid as blind. No, they did not represent him as blind, but only blind folded, which undoubtedly leaves the impression that the love-god may peep under the bandage; and we advise all young people to take advantage of that trick—look before you love. History has proven that persons of the same temperament should not marry, for their children are apt to inherit the *bad* qualities of each parent; while upon the other hand, when opposites marry the children are apt to inherit the *good* qualities of each parent.

Marriage is the most important step taken in life. When a young man goes out into the world to seek fame and fortune the energies of his mind are apt to concentrate upon the problem of obtaining a large fortune. The wife is thought of as a convenience, the love-god is consulted and fancy rules the occasion. Now let me say to all young men, the family is the great object of life. You may pile millions together, and it is all scattered as soon as you are dead. A man's children are his only living and permanent representatives.

You should not therefore consult fancy with regard to fortune or other trivial things, but in the name of all the gods, at once consult common sense in regard to the family you produce.

While Don's friend was upon the tour of inquiry to ascertain the identity of the handsome young lady, Don sat alone upon a log, and said mentally, "A woman may draw me out of the sea ten thousand times, and she would never look like that young lady. O! God, who can she be! Perhaps out of my reach." Don's friend returned smiling. "Lucky, lucky," and Don's friend concluded with a laugh. "What now?" said Don, impatiently.

"That lady is the girl that drew Don Carlo out of the river, her name is Suza Fairfield, and she is the belle of Port William. An orphan girl raised and educated by old Aunt Katy Demitt. She has had a number of suitors, but has never consented to leave Aunt Katy's house as a free woman."

When the congregation dispersed in the evening, Don Carlo and Suza Fairfield rode side by side toward Port William.

The language of courtship is seldom recorded. The ever open ear of the Angel of observation, has only furnished us with these words:

"You are old, my liege, slightly touched with gray. Pray let me live and with Aunt Katy stay."

"With old Aunt Katy you shall live my dear, and on her silent grave drop a weeping tear."

We can only speak of Suza Fairfield as we wish to speak of all other belles.

> The outward acts of every belle,
> Her inward thoughts reveal;
> And by this rule she tries to tell
> How other people feel.

It was the neighborhood talk, that Suza Fairfield, the

belle of Port William, and Don Carlo, the hero of Shirt-Tail Bend, were engaged to be married.

All neighborhoods will talk. Aunt Katy at the table, Betsey Green and Cousin Sally; the meeting and the show; all neighborhoods will talk, for God has made them so.

Secrets should be kept, but neighbors let them go; with caution on the lip, they let a neighbor know, all secrets here below. Some add a little and some take away. Each believes his neighbors in everything they say. They hold a secret *sacred* and only tell a friend, and then whisper in the ear, Sally told me this and you must keep it dear; when all have kept it and every body knows, true or false, they tell it as it goes.

SCENE SIXTH.—THE SECOND GENERATION.

> The son may wear the father's crown,
> When the gray old father's dead;
> May wear his shoe, and wear his gown,
> But he can never wear his head.

How few realize that we are so swiftly passing away, and giving our places on earth, to new men and women.

Tramp, tramp, tramp, and on we go, from the cradle to the grave, without stopping to reflect, that an old man is passing away every hour, and a new one taking his place.

Like drops of rain, descending upon the mountains, and hurrying down to form the great river, running them off to the ocean, and then returning in the clouds. The change is almost imperceptible.

New men come upon the stage of life as it were unobserved, and old ones pass away in like manner, and thus the great river of life flows on. Were the change sudden, and all at once, it would shock the philosophy of the human race. A few men live to witness the rise and fall of two generations. Long years have intervened and the characters portrayed in the preceding part of our story, have all passed away.

Some of their descendants come upon the stage to fight the great battle of life.

Young Simon will first claim our attention; he is the only son of S. S. Simon by a second wife, his mother is dead, and Young Simon is heir to a large estate.

The decade from eighteen hundred and forty to eighteen

hundred and fifty, is, perhaps, the most interesting decade in the history of the settlement and progress of the Western States.

In that era, the great motive power of our modern civilization, the iron horse and the magnetic telegraph were put into successful operation, across the broad and beautiful Western States.

The history of the West and Southwest in the first half of the nineteenth century, is replete with romance, or with truth stranger than fiction. The sudden rise of a moneyed aristocracy in the West, furnishes a theme for the pen of a historian of no mean ability.

This American aristocracy, diverse from the aristocracy of the old world, who stimulated by family pride, preserved the history of a long line of ancestors, born to distinction, and holding the tenure of office by inheritance, could trace the heroic deeds of their fathers back to the dark ages, while some of our American aristocrats are unable to give a true history of their grandfather.

In the first half of the nineteeth century the cultivation of the cotton plant in the Southern States assumed gigantic proportions. The Northern States bartered their slaves for money, and the forest of the great Mississippi river fell by the ax of the colored man; salvation from the *demons* of *want* was preached by the nigger and the mule.

Young Simon was a cotton planter, inheriting from his father four plantations of one thousand acres, and more than six hundred slaves.

Young Simon knew very little of the history of his family, and the more he learned of it, the less he wanted to know. His father in his lifetime, had learned the history of Roxie Daymon *alias* Roxie Fairfield, up to the time she left Louisville, and had good reason to believe that Roxie Daymon, or her descendants, also Suza Fairfield, or her descendants still survived. But as we have said, S. S. Simon stood in the half-way-house, between the honest man and the rogue. He reflected upon the subject mathematically, as he said mentally, "Twenty thousand dollars and twenty years interest—why! it would break me up; I wish to die a *rich man*."

And onward he strove, seasoned to hardship in early life, he slept but little, the morning bell upon his plantations sounded its iron notes up and down the Mississippi long before daylight every morning, that the slaves might be ready to resume their work as soon as they could see. Simon's anxiety to die a *rich man* had so worked upon his feelings for twenty years, that he was a hard master and a keen financier.

The time to die never entered his brain; for it was all absorbed with the *die rich* question. Unexpectedly to him, death's white face appeared when least expected, from hard work, and exposure, S. S. Simon was taken down with the *swamp fever;* down—down—down for a few days and then the *crisis*, the last night of his suffering was terrible, the attending physician and his only son stood by his bedside. All night he was delirious, everything he saw was in the shape of Roxie Daymon, every movement made about the bed, the dying man would cry, "*Take Roxie Daymon away.*"

Young Simon was entirely ignorant of his father's history —and the name *Roxie Daymon* made a lasting impression on his brain. Young Simon grew up without being inured to any hardships, and his health was not good, for he soon followed his father; during his short life he had everything that heart could desire, except a family name and good health, the lack of which made him almost as poor as the meanest of his slaves.

Young Simon received some comfort in his last days from his cousin Cæsar. Cæsar Simon was the son of the brother of S. S. Simon who died in early life, leaving three children in West Tennessee. Cousin Cæsar was raised by two penniless sisters, whom he always called "big-sis" and "little-sis." "Big-sis" was so called from being the eldest, and had the care of cousin Cæsar's childhood. Cousin Cæsar manifested an imaginary turn of mind in early childhood. He was, one day, sitting on his little stool, by the side of the tub in which "big-sis" was washing, (for she was a washer-woman,) gazing intently upon the surface of the water. "What in the world are you looking at C-a-e-s-a-r?" said the woman, straightening up in astonishment.

"Looking at them bubbles on the suds," said the boy, gravely.

"And what of the bubbles?" continued the woman.

"I expected to see one of them burst into a l-o-a-f of b-r-e-a-d," said the child honestly.

"Big-sis" took cousin Cæsar to the fire, went to the cupboard and cut her last loaf of bread, and spread upon it the last mouthful of butter she had in the world, and gave it cousin Cæsar.

And thus he received his first lesson of reward for imagination which, perhaps, had something to do with his after life.

Cousin Cæsar detested work, but had a disposition to see the bottom of everything. No turkey-hen or guinea fowl could make a nest that cousin Cæsar could not find. He grew up mischievous, so much so that "big-sis" would occasionally thrash him. He would then run off and live with "little-sis" until "little-sis" would better the instruction, for she would whip also. He would then run back to live with "big-sis." In this way cousin Cæsar grew to thirteen years of age—too big to whip. He then went to live with old Smith, who had a farm on the Tennessee river, containing a large tract of land, and who hired a large quantity of steam wood cut every season. Rob Roy was one of old Smith's wood cutters—a bachelor well advanced in years, he lived alone in a cabin made of poles, on old Smith's land. His sleeping couch was made with three poles, running parallel with the wall of the cabin, and filled with straw. He never wore any stockings and seldom wore a coat, winter or summer. The furniture in his cabin consisted of a three-legged stool, and a pine goods box. His ax was a handsome tool, and the only thing he always kept brightly polished. He was a good workman at his profession of cutting wood. No one knew anything of his history. He was a man that seldom talked; he was faithful to work througn the week, but spent the Sabbath day drinking whisky. He went to the village every Saturday evening and purchased one gallon of whisky, which he carried in a stone jug to his cabin, and drank it all himself by Monday morning, when he would be ready to go to work again. Old Rob Roy's habits haunted the mind of cousin Cæsar, and he resolved to play a trick upon the old wood cutter. Old Smith had some *hard cider* to which cousin Cæsar had access. One lonesome Sunday cousin Cæsar stole Roy's jug half full of whisky, poured the whisky out, re-filled the jug with cider, and cautiously slipped it back into Roy's cabin. On Monday morning Rob Roy refused to work, and was very mad. Old Smith demanded to know the cause of the trouble. "You can't fool a man with *cider* who loves good *whisky*," said Roy indignantly. Old Smith traced the trick up and discharged cousin Cæsar.

At twenty years of age we find Cousin Cæsar in Paducah, Kentucky, calling himself Cole Conway, in company with one Steve Sharp—they were partners—in the game, as they called it. In the back room of a saloon, dimly lighted, one dark night, another party, more proficient in the sleight of hand, had won the last dime in their possession. The time had come to close up. The sun had crossed the meridian on the other side of the globe. Cole Conway and Steve Sharp crawled into an old straw shed, in the suburbs, of the village, and were soon soundly sleeping. The sun had silvered the old straw shed when Sharp awakened, and saw Conway sitting up, as white as death's old horse. "What on earth is the matter, Conway?" said Sharp, inquiringly.

"I slumbered heavy in the latter end of night, and had a brilliant dream, and awoke from it, to realize this old straw shed doth effect me," said Conway gravely. "The dream! the dream!" demanded Sharp. "I dreamed that we were playing cards, and I was dealing out the deck; the last card was mine, and it was very thick. Sharp, it looked like a box, and with thumb and finger I pulled it open. In it there were three fifty-dollar gold pieces, four four-dollar gold pieces, and ten one-dollar gold pieces. I put the money in my pocket, and was listening for you to claim half, as you purchased the cards. You said nothing more than that 'them cards had been put up for men who sell prize cards.' I took the money out again, when lo, and behold! one of the fifty-dollar pieces had turned to a rule about eight inches long, hinged in the middle. Looking at it closely I saw small letters engraved upon it, which I was able to read—you know, Sharp, I learned to read by spelling the names on steamboats—or that is the way I learned the letters of the alphabet. The inscription directed me to a certain place, and there I would find a steam carriage that could be run on any common road where carriages are drawn by horses. We went, and found the carriage. It was a beautiful carriage—with highly finished box—on four wheels, the box was large enough for six persons to sit on the inside. The pilot sat upon the top, steering with a wheel, the engineer, who was also fireman, and the engine, sat on the aft axle, behind the passenger box. The whole structure was very light, the boiler was of polished brass, and sat upon end. The heat was engendered by a chemical combination of phosphorus and tinder. The golden rule gave directions how to run the engine—by my directions, Sharp, you was pilot and I was engineer, and we started south, toward my old home. People came running out from houses and fields to see us pass I saw something on the beautiful brass boiler that looked like a slide door. I shoved it, and it slipped aside, revealing the dial of a clock which told the time of day, also by a separate hand and figures, told the speed at which the carriage was running. On the right hand side of the dial I saw the figures 77. They were made of India rubber, and hung upon two brass pins. I drew the slide door over the dial except when I wished to look at the time of day, or the rate of speed at which we were running, and every time I opened the door, one of the figure 7's had fallen off the pin. I would replace it, and again find it fallen off. So I concluded it was only safe to run seven miles an hour, and I regulated to that speed. In a short time, I looked again, and we were running at the rate of fifteen miles an hour. I knew that I had not altered the gauge of steam. A hissing sound caused me to think the water was getting low in the boiler. On my left I saw a brass handle that resembled the handle of a pump. I seized it and commenced work. I could hear the bubbling of the water. I look down at the dry road, and said, mentally, 'no water can come from there.' Oh! how I trembled. It so frightened me that I found myself wide awake."

"Dreams are but eddies in the current of the mind, which cut off from reflection's gentle stream, sometimes play strange, fantastic tricks. I have tumbled headlong down from high and rocky cliffs; cold-blooded snakes have crawled 'round my limbs; the worms that eat through dead men's flesh, have crawled upon my skin, and I have dreamed of transportation beyond the shores of time. My last night's dream hoisted me beyond my hopes, to let me fall and find myself in this d—— old straw shed." "The devil never dreams," said Sharp, coolly, and then continued; "Holy men of old dreamed of the Lord, but never of the devil, and to understand a dream, we must be just to all the world, and to ourselves before God."

"I have a proposition to make to you, Conway?"

"*What?*" said Conway, eagerly.

"If you will tell me in confidence, your true name and history, I will give you mine," said Sharp, emphatically. "Agreed," said Conway, and then continued, "as you made he proposition give us yours first."

"My name is Steve Brindle. My father was called Brindle Bill, and once lived in Shirt-Tail Bend, on the Mississippi. He died in the state prison. My mother was a sister of Sundown Hill, who lived in the same neighborhood. My father and mother were never married. So you see, I am a come by-chance, and I have been going by chance all of my life. Now, I have told you the God's truth, so far as I know it. Now make a clean breast of it, Conway, and let us hear your pedigree," said Brindle, confidentially.

"I was born in Tennessee. My father's name was Cæsar Simon, and I bear his name. My mother's name was Nancy Wade. I do not remember either of them. I was partly raised by my sisters, and the balance of the time I have tried to raise myself, but it seems it will take me a long time to *make a raise*—" at this point, Brindle interfered in breathless suspense, with the inquiry, "Did you have an uncle named S. S. Simon?" "I have heard my sister say as much," continued Simon.

"Then your dream is interpreted," said Brindle, emphatically. "Your Uncle, S. S. Simon, has left one of the largest estates in Arkansas, and now you are on the steam wagon again," said Brindle, slapping his companion on the shoulder.

Brindle had been instructed by his mother, and made

Cousin Cæsar acquainted with the outline of all the history detailed in this narrative, except the history of Roxie Daymon *alias* Roxie Fairfield, in Chicago.

The next day the two men were hired as hands to go down the river on a flat-bottom boat.

Roxie Daymon, whose death has been recorded, left an only daughter, now grown to womanhood, and bearing her mother's name. Seated in the parlor of one of the descendants of Aunt Patsy Perkins, in Chicago, we see her sad, and alone; we hear the hall bell ring. A servant announces the name of Gov. Morock. "Show the Governor up," said Roxie, sadly. The ever open ear of the Angel of observation has only furnished us with the following conversation:

"Everything is positively lost, madam, not a cent in the world. Every case has gone against us, and no appeal, madam. You are left hopelessly destitute, and penniless. Daymon should have employed me ten years ago—but now, it is too late. Everything is gone, madam," and the Governor paused. "My mother was once a poor, penniless girl, and I can bear it too," said Roxie, calmly. "But you see," said the Governor, softening his voice; "you are a handsome young lady; your fortune is yet to be made. For fifty dollars, madam, I can fix you up a *shadow*, that will marry you off. You see the law has some *loop holes* and—and in your case, madam, it is no harm to take one; no harm, no harm, madam," and the Governor paused again. Roxie looked at the man sternly, and said: "I have no further use for a lawyer, Sir." "Any business hereafter, madam, that you may wish transacted, send your card to No. 77, Strait street," and the Governor made a side move toward the door, touched the rim of his hat and disappeared.

It was in the golden month of October, and calm, smoky days of Indian summer, that a party of young people living in Chicago, made arrangements for a pleasure trip to

New Orleans. There were four or five young ladies in the party, and Roxie Daymon was one. She was handsome and interesting—if her fortune *was gone*. The party consisted of the moneyed aristocracy of the city, with whom Roxie had been raised and educated. Every one of the party was willing to contribute and pay Roxie's expenses, for the sake of her company. A magnificent steamer, of the day, plying between St. Louis and New Orleans, was selected for the carrier, three hundred feet in length, and sixty feet wide. The passenger cabin was on the upper deck, nearly two hundred feet in length; a guard eight feet wide, for a footway, and promenade on the outside of the hall, extended on both sides, the full length of the cabin; a plank partition divided the long hall—the aft room was the ladies', the front the gentlemen's cabin. The iron horse, or some of his successors, will banish these magnificent floating palaces, and I describe, for the benefit of coming generations.

Nothing of interest occured to our party, until the boat landed at the Simon plantations. Young Simon and cousin Cæsar boarded the boat, for passage to New Orleans, for they were on their way to the West Indies, to spend the winter. Young Simon was in the last stage of consumption and his physician had recommended the trip as the last remedy. Young Simon was walking on the outside guard, opposite the ladies' cabin, when a female voice with a shrill and piercing tone rang upon his ear—"*Take Roxie Daymon away.*" The girls were romping. — " Take Roxie Daymon away,'' were the mysterious dying words of young Simon's father. Simon turned, and mentally bewildered, entered the gentlemen's cabin. A colored boy, some twelve years of age, in the service of the boat, was passing—Simon held a silver dollar in his hand as he said, "I will give you this, if you will ascertain and point out to me the lady in the cabin, that they call *Roxie Daymon.*" The imp of Africa seized the coin, and passing on said in a voice too low for Simon's ear, "good bargain, boss." The Roman Eagle was running down stream through the dark and muddy waters of the Mississippi, at the rate of twenty miles an hour.

In the dusk of the evening, Young Simon and Roxie Daymon were sitting side by side—alone, on the aft-guard of the boat. The ever open ear of the Angel of observation has furnished us with the following conversation.

"Your mother's maiden name, is what I am anxious to learn," said Simon gravely.

"Roxie Fairfield, an orphan girl, raised in Kentucky." said Roxie sadly.

"Was she an only child, or did she have sisters?" said Simon inquiringly.

"My mother died long years ago—when I was too young to remember, my father had no relations—that I ever heard of—Old aunt Patsey Perkins—a great friend of mother's in her life-time, told me after mother was dead, and I had grown large enough to think about kinsfolk, that mother had two sisters somewhere, named Rose and Suza, *poor trash*, as she called them; and that is all I know of my relations: and to be frank with you, I am nothing but poor trash too, I have no family history to boast of," said Roxie honestly.

"You will please excuse me Miss, for wishing to know something of your family history—there is a mystery connected with it, that may prove to your advantage"—Simon was *convinced.*—He pronounced the word twenty—when the Angel of caution placed his finger on his lip—*hush!*—and young Simon turned the conversation, and as soon as he could politely do so, left the presence of the young lady, and sought cousin Cæsar, who by the way, was well acquainted with the most of the circumstances we have recorded, but had wisely kept them to himself. Cousin Cæsar now told young Simon the whole story.

Twenty-thousand dollars, with twenty years interest, was against his estate. Roxie Daymon, the young lady on the boat, was an heir, others lived in Kentucky—all of which cousin Cæsar learned from a descendant of Brindle Bill. The pleasure party with Simon and cousin Cæsar, stopped at the same hotel in the Crescent City. At the end of three weeks the pleasure party returned to Chicago. Young Simon and cousin Cæsar left for the West Indies.—Young Simon and Roxie Daymon were engaged to be married the following spring at Chicago. Simon saw many beautiful women in his travels—but the image of Roxie Daymon was ever before him. The good Angel of observation has failed to inform us, of Roxie Daymon's feelings and object in the match. A young and beautiful woman; full of life and vigor consenting to wed a dying man, *hushed* the voice of the good Angel, and he has said nothing.

Spring with its softening breezes returned—the ever to be remembered spring of 1861.

The shrill note of the iron horse announced the arrival of young Simon and cousin Cæsar in Chicago, on the 7th day of April, 1861.

Simon had lived upon excitement, and reaching the destination of his hopes—the great source of his life failed—cousin Cæsar carried him into the hotel—he never stood alone again—the marriage was put off—until Simon should be better. On the second day, cousin Cæsar was preparing to leave the room, on business in a distant part of the city. Roxie had been several times alone with Simon, and was then present. Roxie handed a sealed note to cousin Cæsar, politely asking him to deliver it. The note was inscribed, Gov. Morock, No. 77 Strait street.

Cousin Cæsar had been absent but a short time, when that limb of the law appeared and wrote a will dictated by young Simon; bequeathing all of his possessions, without reserve to Roxie Daymon. "How much," said Roxie, as the Governor was about to leave. "Only ten dollars, madam," said the Governor, as he stuffed the bill carelessly in his vest pocket and departed.

Through the long vigils of the night cousin Cæsar sat by the side of the dying man; before the sun had silvered the eastern horizon, the soul of young Simon was with his fathers. The day was consumed in making preparations for the last honor due the dead. Cousin Cæsar arranged with a party to take the remains to Arkansas, and place the son by the side of the father, on the home plantation. The next morning as cousin Cæsar was scanning the morning papers, the following brief notice attracted his attention: "Young Simon, the wealthy young cotton planter, who died in the city yesterday, left by his last will and testament his whole estate, worth more than a million of dollars, to Roxie Daymon, a young lady of this city."

Cousin Cæsar was bewildered and astonished. He was a stranger in the city; he rubbed his hand across his forehead to collect his thoughts, and remembered No. 77 Strait street. "Yes I observed it—it is a law office," he said mentally, "there is something in that number seventy-seven, I have never understood it before, since my dream on the steam carriage *seventy-seven*," and cousin Cæsar directed his steps toward Strait street.

"Important business, I suppose sir," said Governor Morock, as he read cousin Cæsar's anxious countenance.

"Yes, somewhat so," said cousin Cæsar, pointing to the notice in the paper, he continued: "I am a relative of Simon and have served him faithfully for two years, and they say he has willed his estate to a stranger."

"Is it p-o-s-s-i-b-l-e-," said the Governor, affecting astonishment.

"What would you advise me to do?" said cousin Cæsar imploringly.

"Break the will—break the will, sir," said the Governor emphatically.

'Ah! that will take money," said cousin Cæsar sadly.

"Yes, yes, but it will bring money," said the Governor, rubbing his hands together.

"I s-u-p p-o-s-e we would be required to prove incapacity on the part of Simon," said cousin Cæsar slowly.

"Money will prove anything," said the Governor decidedly.

The Governor struck the right key, for cousin Cæsar was well schooled in treacherous humanity, and noted for seeing the bottom of things; but he did not see the bottom of the Governor's dark designs.

"How much for this case?" said cousin Cæsar.

"Oh! I am liberal—I am liberal," said the Governor rubbing his hands and continuing, "can't tell exactly, owing to the trouble and cost of the things, as we go along. A million is the stake—well, let me see, this is no child's play. A man that has studied for long years—you can't expect him to be cheap—but as I am in the habit of working for nothing—if you will pay me one thousand dollars in advance, I will undertake the case, and then a few more thousands will round it up—can't say exactly, any more sir, than I am always liberal."

Cousin Caesar had some pocket-money, furnished by young Simon, to pay expenses etc., amounting to a little more than one thousand dollars. His mind was bewildered with the number seventy-seven, and he paid over to the Governor one thousand dollars. After Governor Morock had the money safe in his pocket, he commenced a detail of the cost of the suit—among other items, was a large amount for witnesses.

The Governor had the case—it was a big case—and the Governor has determined to make it pay him.

Cousin Cæser reflected, and saw that he must have help, and as he left the office of Governor Morock, said mentally: "One of them d—n figure sevens I saw in my dream, would fall off the pin, and I fear, I have struck the wrong lead."

In the soft twilight of the evening, when the conductor cried, "all aboard," cousin Cæsar was seated in the train, on his way to Kentucky, to solicit aid from Cliff Carlo, the oldest son and representative man, of the family descended from Don Carlo, the hero of Shirt-Tail Bend, and Suza Fairfield, the belle of Port William.

SCENE SEVENTH—WAR BETWEEN THE STATES.

The late civil war between the States of the American Union was the inevitable result of two civilizations under one government, which no power on earth could have prevented.

We place the federal and confederate soldier in the same scale *per se*, and one will not weigh the other down an atom. So even will they poise that you may mark the small allowance of the weight of a hair. But place upon the beam the pea of their actions while upon the stage, *on either side*, and the poise may be up or down.

More than this, your orator has nothing to say of the war, except its effect upon the characters we describe.

The bright blossoms of a May morning were opening to meet the sunlight, while the surrounding foliage was waving in the soft breeze of spring; on the southern bank of the beautiful Ohio, where the momentous events of the future were concealed from the eyes of the preceding generation by the dark veil of the coming revolutions of the globe.

We see Cousin Cæsar and Cliff Carlo in close counsel, upon the subject of meeting the expenses of the contest at law over the Simon estate, in the State of Arkansas

Cliff Carlo was rather non-committal. Roxie Daymon was a near relative, and the unsolved problem in the case of compromise and law did not admit of haste on the part of the Carlo family. Compromise was not the forte of Cousin Cæsar. To use his own words, "I have made the cast, and will stand the hazard of the die."

But the enterprise, with surrounding circumstances, would have baffled a bolder man than Cæsar Simon. The first gun of the war had been fired at Fort Sumter, in South Carolina, on the 12th day of April, 1861.

The President of the United States had called for seventy-five thousand war-like men to redezvous at Washington City, and form a *Prætorian* guard, to strengthen the arm of the government. *To arms, to arms!* was the cry both North and South. The last lingering hope of peace between the States had faded from the minds of all men, and the bloody crest of war was painted on the horizon of the future. The border slave States, in the hope of peace, had remained inactive all winter. They now withdrew from the Union and joined their fortunes with the South, except Kentucky—the *dark and bloody ground* historic in the annals of war—showed the *white feather*, and announced to the world that her soil was the holy ground of peace. This proclamation was *too thin* for Cæsar Simon. Some of the Carlo family had long since immigrated to Missouri. To consult with them on the will affair, and meet with an element more disposed to defend his prospect of property, Cousin Cæsar left Kentucky for Missouri. On the fourth day of July, 1861, in obedience to the call of the President, the Congress of the United States met at Washington City. This Congress called to the contest five hundred thousand men; *"cried havoc and let slip the dogs of war,"* and Missouri was invaded by federal troops, who were subsequently put under the command of Gen. Lyon. About the middle of July we see Cousin Cæsar marching in the army of Gen. Sterling Price—an army composed of all classes of humanity, who rushed to the conflict without promise of pay or assistance from the government of the Confederate States of America—an army without arms or equipment, except such as it gathered from the citizens, double-barreled shot-guns—an army of volunteers without the promise of pay or hope of reward; composed of men from eighteen to seventy years of age, with a uniform of costume varying from the walnut colored roundabout to the pigeon-tailed broadcloth coat. The mechanic and the farmer, the professional and the non-professional, the merchant and the jobber, the speculator and the butcher, the country schoolmaster and the printer's devil, the laboring man and the dead-beat, all rushed into Price's army, seemingly under the influence of the watchword of the old Jews, "*To your tents, O Israel!*" and it is a fact worthy of record that this unarmed and untrained army never lost a battle on Missouri soil in the first year of the war.* Gov. Jackson had fled from Jefferson City on the approach of the federal army, and assembled the Legislature at Neosho, in the southwest corner of the State, who were unable to assist Price's army. The troops went into the field, thrashed the wheat and milled it for themselves; were often upon half rations, and frequently lived upon roasting ears. Except the Indian or border war in Kentucky, fought by a preceding generation, the first year of the war in Missouri is unparalleled in the history of war on this continent. Gen. Price managed to subsist an army without governmental resources. His men were never demoralized for the want of food, pay or clothing, and were always cheerful, and frequently danced 'round their camp-fires, bare-footed and ragged, with a spirit of merriment that would put the blush upon the cheek of a circus. Gen. Price wore nothing upon his shoulders but a brown linen duster, and, his white hair streaming in the breeze on the field of battle, was a picture resembling the *war-god* of the Romans in ancient fable.

This army of ragged heroes marched over eight hundred miles on Missouri soil, and seldom passed a week without an engagement of some kind—it was confined to no particular

---

*The so called battle of Boonville was a rash venture of citizens, not under the command of Gen. Price at the time.

line of operations, but fought the enemy wherever they found him. It had started on the campaign without a dollar, without a wagon, without a cartridge, and without a bayonet-gun; and when it was called east of the Missisippi river, it possessed about eight thousand bayonet-guns, fifty pieces of cannon, and four hundred tents, taken almost exclusively from the Federals, on the hard-fought fields of battle.

When this army crossed the Mississippi river the star of its glory had set never to rise again. The invigorating name of *state rights* was *merged* in the Southern Confederacy.

With this prelude to surrounding circumstances, we will now follow the fortunes of Cousin Cæsar. Enured to hardships in early life, possessing a penetrating mind and a selfish disposition, Cousin Cæsar was ever ready to float on the stream of prosperity, with triumphant banners, or go down as *drift wood*.

And whatever he may have lacked in manhood, he was as brave as a lion on the battle-field; and the campaign of Gen. Price in Missouri suited no private soldier better than Cæsar Simon. Like all soldiers in an active army, he thought only of battle and amusement. Consequently, the will, Gov. Morock and the Simon estate occupied but little of Cousin Cæsar's reflections. One idea had taken possession of him, and that was southern victory. He enjoyed the triumphs of his fellow soldiers, and ate his roasting ears with the same invigorating spirit. A sober second thought and cool reflections only come with the struggle for his own life, and with it a self-reproach that always, sooner or later, overtakes the faithless.

The battle of Oak Hill, usually called the battle of Springfield, was one of the hardest battles fought west of the Mississippi river. The federal troops, under Gen. Lyon, amounted to nearly ten thousand men. The confederate troops, under Generals McCulloch, Price, and Pearce, were about eleven thousand men.

On the ninth of August the Confederates camped at Wilson's Creek, intending to advance upon the Federals at Springfield. The next morning General Lyon attacked them before sunrise. The battle was fought with rash bravery on both sides. General Lyon, after having been twice wounded, was shot dead while leading a rash charge. Half the loss on the Confederate side was from Price's army—a sad memorial of the part they took in the contest. Soon after the fall of General Lyon the Federals retreated to Springfield, and left the Confederates master of the field. About the closing scene of the last struggle, Cousin Cæsar received a musket ball in the right leg, and fell among the wounded and dying.

The wound was not necessarily fatal; no bone was broken, but it was very painful and bleeding profusely. When Cousin Cæsar, after lying a long time where he fell, realized the situation, he saw that without assistance he must bleed to death; and impatient to wait for some one to pick him up, he sought quarters by his own exertions. He had managed to crawl a quarter of a mile, and gave out at a point where no one would think of looking for the wounded. Weak from the loss of blood, he could crawl no farther. The light of day was only discernable in the dim distance of the West; the Angel of silence had spread her wing over the bloody battle field. In vain Cousin Cæsar pressed his hand upon the wound; the crimson life would ooze out between his fingers, and Cousin Cæsar lay down to die. It was now dark; no light met his eye, and no sound came to his ear, save the song of two grasshoppers in a cluster of bushes—one sang "Katie-did!" and the other sang "Katie-didn't!" Cousin Cæsar said, mentally, "It will soon be decided with me whether Katie did or whether she didn't! In the last moments of hope Cousin Cæsar heard and recognized the sound of a human voice, and gathering all the strength of his lungs, pronounced the word—"S-t-e-v-e!" In a short time he saw two men approaching him. It was Steve Brindle and a Cherokee Indian. As soon as they saw the situation, the Indian darted like a wild deer to where there had been a camp fire, and returned with his cap full of ashes which he applied to Cousin Cæsar's wound. Steve Brindle bound it up and stopped the blood. The two men then carried the wounded man to camp—to recover and reflect upon the past. Steve Brindle was a private, in the army of General Pearce, from Arkansas, and the Cherokee Indian was a camp follower belonging to the army of General McCulloch. They were looking over the battle field in search of their missing friends, when they accidentally discovered and saved Cousin Cæsar.

Early in the month of September, Generals McCulloch and Price having disagreed on the plan of campaign, General Price announced to his officers his intention of moving north, and required a report of effective men in his army. A lieutenant, after canvassing the company to which Cousin Cæsar belonged, went to him as the last man. Cousin Cæsar reported ready for duty. "All right, you are the last man— No. 77," said the lieutenant, hastily, leaving Cousin Cæsar to his reflections. "There is that number again; what can it mean? Marching north, perhaps to meet a large force, is our company to be reduced to seven? One of them d——d figure sevens would fall off and one would be left on the pin. How should it be counted—s-e-v-e-n or half? Set up two guns and take one away, half would be left; enlist two men, and if one is killed, half would be left—yet, with these d——d figures, when you take one you only have one eleventh part left. Cut by the turn of fortune; cut with short rations; cut with a musket ball; cut by self-reproach—*ah, that's the deepest cut of all!*" said Cousin Cæsar, mentally, as he retired to the tent.

Steve Brindle had saved Cousin Cæsar's life, had been an old comrade in many a hard game, had divided his last cent with him in many hard places, had given him his family history and opened the door for him to step into the palace of wealth. Yet, when Cousin Cæsar was surrounded with wealth and power, when honest employment would, in all human possibility, have redeemed his old comrade, Cousin Cæsar, willing to conceal his antecedents, did not know S-t-e-v-e Brindle.

General Price reached the Missouri river, at Lexington, on the 12th of September, and on the 20th captured a Federal force intrenched there, under the command of Colonel Mulligan, from whom he obtained five cannon, two mortars and over three thousand bayonet guns. In fear of large Federal forces north of the Missouri river, General Price retreated south. Cousin Cæsar was again animated with the spirit of war and had dismissed the superstitious fear of 77 from his mind. He continued his amusements 'round the camp fires in Price's army, as he said, mentally, "Governor Morock will keep things straight, at his office on Strait street, in Chicago."

Roxie Daymon had pleasantly passed the summer and fall on the reputation of being *rich*, and was always the toast in the fashionable parties of the upper-ten in Chicago. During the first year of the war it was emphatically announced by the government at Washington, that it would never interfere with the slaves of loyal men. Roxie Daymon was loyal and lived in a loyal city. It was war times, and Roxie had received no dividends from the Simon estate.

In the month of January, 1862, the cold north wind from the lakes swept the dust from the streets in Chicago, and seemed to warn the secret, silent thoughts of humanity of the great necessity of m-o-n-e-y.

The good Angel of observation saw Roxie Daymon, with

a richly-trimmed fur cloak upon her shoulders and hands muffed, walking swiftly on Strait street, in Chicago, watching the numbers—at No. 77 she disappeared.

The good Angel opened his ear and has furnished us with the following conversation:

"I have heard incidentally that Caesar Simon is preparing to break the will of my *esteemed* friend, Young Simon, of Arkansas," said Roxie, sadly.

"Is it p-o-s s-i-b-l e?" said Governor Morock, affecting astonishment, and then continued, "More work for the lawyers, you know I am always liberal, madam." "But do you think it possible?" said Roxie, inquiringly. "You have money enough to fight with, madam, money enough to fight," said the Governor, decidedly. "I suppose we will have to prove that Simon was in full possession of his mental faculties at the time," said Roxie, with legal *acumen*. "Certainly, certainly madam, money will prove anything; will prove anything, madam," said the Governor, rubbing his hands. "I believe you were the only person present at the time," said Roxie, honestly.

"I am always liberal, madam, a few thousands will arrange the testimony, madam. Leave that to me, if you please," and in a softer tone of voice the Governor continued, "you ought to pick up the *crumbs*, madam, pick up the crumbs." "I would like to do so for I have never spent a cent in the prospect of the estate, though my credit is good for thousands in this city. I want to see how a dead man's shoes will fit before I wear them," said Roxie, sadly.

"Good philosophy, madam, good philosophy," said the Governor, and continued to explain. "There is cotton on the bank of the river at the Simon plantations. Some arrangement ought to be made, and I think I could do it through some officer of the federal army," said the Governor, rubbing his hand across his forehead, and continued, "that's what I mean by picking up the crumbs, madam."

"*How much?*" said Roxie, preparing to leave the office.

"I am always liberal, madam, always liberal. Let me see; it is attended with some difficulty; can't leave the city; too much business pressing (rubbing his hands); well—well —I will pick up the crumbs for half. Think I can secure two or three hundred bales of cotton, madam," said the Governor, confidentially.

"How much is a bale of cotton worth?" said Roxie, affecting ignorance.

"Only four hundred dollars, madam; nothing but a crumb—nothing but a crumb, madam," said the Governor, in a tone of flattery.

"Do the best you can," said Roxie, in a confidential tone, as she left the office.

Governor Morock was enjoying the reputation of the fashionable lawyer among the upper-ten in Chicago. Roxie Daymon's good sense condemned him, but she did not feel at liberty to break the line of association.

Cliff Carlo did nothing but write a letter of inquiry to Governor Morock, who informed him that the Simon estate was worth more than a million and a quarter, and that m-o-n-e-y would *break the will.*

The second year of the war burst the bubble of peace in Kentucky. The State was invaded on both sides. The clang of arms on the soil where the heroes of a preceding generation slept, called the martial spirits in the shades of Kentucky to rise and shake off the delusion that peace and plenty breed cowards. Cliff Carlo, and many others of the brave sons of Kentucky, united with the southern armies, and fully redeemed their war like character, as worthy descendents of the heroes of the *dark and bloody ground.*

Cliff Carlo passed through the struggles of the war without a sick day or the pain of a wound. We must, therefore, follow the fate of the less fortunate Cæsar Simon.

During the winter of the first year of the war, Price's army camped on the southern border of Missouri.

On the third day of March, 1862, Maj. Gen. Earl Van Dorn, of the Confederate government, assumed the command of the troops under Price and McCulloch, and on the seventh day of March attacked the Federal forces under Curtis and Sturgis, twenty-five thousand strong, at Elkhorn, Van Dorn commanding about twenty thousand men.

Price's army constituted the left and center, with McCulloch on the right. The fight was long and uncertain. About two o'clock McCulloch fell, and his forces failed to press the contest.

The Federals retreated in good order, leaving the Confederates master of the situation.

For some unaccountable decision on the part of Gen. Van Dorn, a retreat of the southern army was ordered, and instead of pursuing the Federals, the wheels of the Southern army were seen rolling south.

Gen. Van Dorn had ordered the sick and disabled many miles in advance of the army. Cousin Cæsar had passed through the conflict safe and sound; it was a camp rumor that Steve Brindle was mortally wounded and sent forward with the sick. The mantle of night hung over Price's army, and the camp fires glimmered in the soft breeze of the evening. Silently and alone Cousin Cæsar stole away from the scene on a mission of love and duty. Poor Steve Brindle had ever been faithful to him, and Cousin Cæsar had suffered self-reproach for his unaccountable neglect of a faithful friend. An opportunity now presented itself for Cousin Cæsar to relieve his conscience and possibly smooth the dying pillow of his faithful friend, Steve Brindle.

Bravely and fearlessly on he sped and arrived at the

camp of the sick. Worn down with the march, Cousin Cæsar never rested until he had looked upon the face of the last sick man. Steve was not there.

Slowly and sadly Cousin Cæsar returned to the army, making inquiry of every one he met for Steve Brindle. After a long and fruitless inquiry, an Arkansas soldier handed Cousin Cæsar a card, saying, "I was requested by a soldier in our command to hand this card to the man whose name it bears, in Price's army." Cousin Cæsar took the card and read, "Csæar Simon—No. 77 deserted." Cousin Cæsar threw the card down as though it was nothing, as he said mentally, "What can it mean. There are those d—d figures again. Steve knew nothing of No. 77 in Chicago. How am I to understand this? Steve understood my ideas of the mysterious No. 77 on the steam carriage. Steve has deserted and takes this plan to inform me. *Ah! that is it!* Steve has couched the information in language that no one can understand but myself. Two of us were on the carriage and two figure *sevens*; one would fall off the pin. Steve has fallen off. He knew I would understand his card when no one else could. But did Steve only wish me to understand that he had left, or did he wish me to follow?" was a problem Cousin Cæsar was unable to decide. It was known to Cousin Cæsar that the Cherokee Indian who, in company with Steve, saved his life at Springfield, had, in company with some of his race, been brought upon the stage of war by Albert Pike. Deserted! And Cousin Cæsar was left alone, with no bosom friend save the friendship of one southern soldier for another. And the idea of *desertion* entered the brain of Cæsar Simon for the first time.

Cæsar Simon was a born soldier, animated by the clang of arms and roar of battle, and although educated in the school of treacherous humanity, he was one of the few who resolved to die in the last ditch, and he concluded his reflections with the sarcastic remark, "Steve Brindle is a coward."

Before Gen. Van Dorn faced the enemy again, he was called east of the Mississippi river. Price's army embarked at Des Arc, on White river, and when the last man was on board the boats, there were none more cheerful than Cousin Cæsar. He was going to fight on the soil of his native State, for it was generally understood the march by water was to Memphis, Tennessee.

It is said that a portion of Price's army showed the *white feather* at Iuka. Cousin Cæsar was not in that division of the army. After that event he was a camp lecturer, and to him the heroism of the army owes a tribute in memory for the brave hand to hand fight in the streets of Corinth, where, from house to house and within a stone's throw of Rosecrans' headquarters, Price's men made the Federals fly. But the Federals were reinforced from their outposts, and Gen. Van Dorn was in command, and the record says he made a rash attack and a hasty retreat.

Maj. Gen. T. C. Hindman was the southern commander of what was called the district of Arkansas west of the Mississippi river. He was a petty despot as well as an unsuccessful commander of an army. The country suffered unparalleled abuses; crops were ravaged, cotton burned, and the magnificent palaces of the southern planter licked up by flames. The torch was applied frequently by an unknown hand. The Southern commander burned cotton to prevent its falling into the hands of the enemy. Straggling soldiers belonging to distant commands traversed the country, robbing the people and burning. How much of this useless destruction is chargable to Confederate or Federal commanders, it is impossible to determine. Much of the waste inflicted upon the country was by the hand of lawless guerrillas. Four hundred bales of cotton were burned on the Simon plantation, and the residence on the home plantation, that cost S. S.

Simon over sixty-five thousand dollars, was nothing but a heap of ashes.

Governor Morock's agents never got any *crumbs*, although the Governor had used nearly all of the thousand dollars obtained from Cousin Cæsar to pick up the *crumbs* on the Simon plantations, he never got a *crumb*.

General Hindman was relieved of his command west of the Mississippi, by President Davis. Generals Kirby, Smith, Holmes and Price subsequently commanded the Southern troops west of the great river. The federals had fortified Helena, a point three hundred miles above Vicksburg on the west bank of the river. They had three forts, with a gun-boat lying in the river, and were about four thousand strong. They were attacked by General Holmes, on the 4th day of July, 1863. General Holmes had under his command General Price's division of infantry, about fourteen hundred men; Fagans brigade of Arkansas, infantry, numbering fifteen hundred men, and Marmaduke's division of Arkansas, and Missouri cavalry, about two thousand, making a total of four thousand and nine hundred men. Marmaduke was ordered to attack the northern fort; Fagan was to attack the southern fort, and General Price the center fort. The onset to be simultaneously and at daylight.

General Price carried his position. Marmaduke and Fagan failed. The gun-boat in the river shelled the captured fort. Price's men sheltered themselves as best they could, awaiting further orders. The scene was alarming above description to Price's men. It was the holiday of American Independence. The failure of their comrades in arms would compel them to retreat under a deadly fire from the enemy. While thus waiting, the turn of battle crouched beneath an old stump. Cousin Cæsar saw in the distance and recognized Steve Brindle, he was a soldier in the federal army.

"Oh treacherous humanity! must I live to learn thee still Steve Brindle fights for m-o-n-e-y?" said Cæsar Simon, mentally. The good Angel of observation whispered in his ear: "Cæsar Simon fights for land *stripped of its ornaments*. Cousin Cæsar scanned the situation and continued to say, mentally: "Life is a sentence of punishment passed by the court of existence on every *private soldier*."

The battle field is the place of execution, and rash commanders are often the executioners. After repeated efforts General Holmes failed to carry the other positions. The retreat of Price's men was ordered; it was accomplished with heavy loss. Cæsar Simon fell, and with him perished the last link in the chain of the Simon family in the male line.

We must now let the curtain fall upon the sad events of the war until the globe makes nearly two more revolutions 'round the sun in its orbit, and then we see the Southern soldiers weary and war-worn—sadly deficient in numbers—lay down their arms—the war is ended. The Angel of peace has spread her golden wing from Maine to Florida, and from Virginia to California. The proclamation of freedom, by President Lincoln, knocked the dollars and cents out of the flesh and blood of every slave on the Simon plantations. Civil courts are in session. The last foot of the Simon land has been sold at sheriff's sale to pay judgments, just and unjust.

> The goose that laid the golden egg
> Has paddled across the river.

Governor Morock has retired from the profession, or the profession has retired from him. He is living on the cheap sale of a bad reputation—that is—all who wish dirty work performed at a low price employ Governor Morock.

Roxie Daymon has married a young mechanic, and is happy in a cottage home. She blots the memory of the past by reading the poem entitled, "The Workman's Saturday Night."

Cliff Carlo is a prosperous farmer in Kentucky and subscriber for

THE ROUGH DIAMOND.

History, Science, Philosophy and Art,

BLENDED IN ORIGINAL LECTURES.

LECTURE I.—LIBERTY AND LAW.

The soul of no sane man was ever so dead, that it could not be aroused from lethargy by the invigorating name of *liberty*.

Human speech has never couched in shape and form any word more sacred to mortal ear than *liberty*.

Dearer than life to the patriotic heart, as expressed by the great American orator when he said, "*Give me liberty or give me death.*"

Strange, but still 'tis true, no philosopher has ever told us what liberty is.

Looking back o'er the dark centuries of the past we observe representative men among all nations arousing the people with the old watch word, *liberty*.

Julius Cæsar, Charlemagne, William the Conqueror, Napoleon Bonaparte, and all great leaders of revolutions, raised the universal cry of oppression and fought under the banner of *liberty*.

All nations have not lived under the same government,

hence it is evident that liberty itself must change with the *times and circumstances.*

When liberty is spoken of every one has an idea of what is meant, for every one has known what it is to live in freedom, and also what it is to live and act *under restraint.*

But then it is obvious, that different persons enjoy liberty according to *circumstances.*

Things that infringe upon the liberty of some, have no such effect upon the liberty of *others.*

So, in a situation where one would feel at liberty, another would feel himself in *bondage.*

Hence it is evident, though all have a general idea of what liberty is, that all have not the same idea of it.

For, as different persons would not all feel free under the same *circumstances,* it follows that liberty itself is not the *same thing at all.*

A man educated in the law feels free in his library, force him to the handles of the plow and he would feel himself in bondage.

> Ah! Liberty—*what is Liberty?*
> The Goddess adored by primitive man,
> In olden times, when justice first began,
> With weights and balances in her hand,
> Reigned triumphant o'er the Grecian land.
> Some ancient sage, the brilliant Goddess saw,
> At first sight lov'd, and changed her name to law,
> And then the duties of domestic life
> Incumbent to her, as to every wife.
> Wooed by millions since that wedding day,
> All of her suitors are compelled to say,
> Individuals must their freedom draw,
> From the union of liberty and law.

But says one, is the universal cry of liberty nothing but a name? is there no such thing as national liberty? There is—all nations have the *inherent right* to make their own laws or in other words to lay the foundation of their own *liberties*.

But as to individual liberty, outside of law, *there is no such thing*.

Law is a universal rule by which the conduct of all is measured, the regulator of society, adopted anciently by kings and rulers, modernly by the people who are the sovereigns of this land.

The first definition of the word law is, power or force; the laws of nature are the result of the power of the unseen hand—the hand of the ruler of *the Universe*.

The laws of society originate with wise and just men, and ripen into the laws of the land; the power of the ruler is the first principle of all law.

The first definition of the word liberty is freedom from restraint, in the union of liberty and law; one is free from restraint as measured by the rule of the law.

To be entirely free from restraint would be enjoyed by few men, and it has been wisely said, "Where there is no law there is no freedom."

Place a man upon an island, solitary and alone—

"And from the center, all round to the sea,
He would be monarch of all he surveyed."

But the moment another man landed upon the island, to have association together, each man would be under restraint.

The force of necessity would compel them to form the blossom of society, and from the customs of society and fruits of association we lay the foundation of the laws of the land.

In all modern nations the people are indirectly the law making power. Public opinion is the blossom of law, for when it is raised sufficiently high its power is *irresistible*.

Charles the First, of England, and Louis the Sixteenth, of France, **could not resist** public opinion.

Justice is the object in view when we appeal to the law, and the proper administration of the law is justice according to law.

While justice is the object of law in the first place, and the proper administration of law in the second place, one may receive justice according to law, but it will be justice only in proportion to the justness of the jaw.

Many things considered just by primitive society fall far short of justice in more advanced civilization.

All nations shape most of their laws according to circumstances, and as time changes or ameliorates circumstances, we say the times have changed and so have the laws.

But says one, if liberty is regulated by *law*, uniform law should produce uniform restraint; or, in other words, under the same laws all should enjoy the same liberties.

Why is it the beggar is drummed out of town for stealing a loaf of bread while the millionaire steals thousands with impunity?

Human laws, unlike divine laws, do not operate of themselves; they are put in force by human hands. Officers of the law like other men are more or less governed by circumstances.

Self and self-preservation is the first law of human nature and few men can stand above the influence of circumstances, and thus *money* has ever ameliorated crime.

When a man who has plenty of *money* breaks the law there are a thousand eyes turned in every direction to find some excuse—every nook and corner is canvassed to pick up something to *palliate the crime.*

But reverse the rule and apply it to the *moneyless man*— no eye is opened by self-interest, or turned round by the greedy love of gold.

> Justice and judges, as cold as the Jews,
> Will meet in the court and give him his dues;
> No plea has been found, since justice began,
> To lie in court for a moneyless man.

While many of our laws are permanent, the administration of them is frequently influenced by the surrounding circumstances.

The laws of human nature and the laws of society frequently come in conflict. Our ideas and natural inclinations are not all free—like individual persons, they are free only according to the laws of the mind.

The laws of the mind govern, to some extent, the actions of men. For we cannot assume that all men are held under restraint only by the laws of society, or the laws of the land.

The laws of organism govern all regulated minds—hence when reason fails to assert authority over the mind, the passions are not under control—they are left free and will grasp satisfaction.

An eminent mental philosopher said, "Man is happy in proportion to the satisfaction of his mental faculties." I should rather say—Man is happy in proportion to the capability of his mind to govern itself.

The laws of organism govern all well regulated minds. The eye is a mental organ of the mind—in fact, it is but the end of a mental nerve, and, if correctly organized, the light is made manifest to the brain—and thus we see. All of our mental organs are like the eye, they receive their influence externally. We are creatures operated upon by circumstances. The savage man belongs to savage circumstances—and the civilized man to civilized circumstances.

The laws of savage life, or human nature, incline all men to dishonesty—it is natural for a man to take advantage of others, to gratify his passions; the laws of civilization is the only restraint.

Universal marriage as soon as maturity arrives, is the natural impulse of youth.

To take possession of anything as soon as it is deserted, or laid aside by another, is the natural impulse of the savage. Honesty, virtue, and manhood all arise from our laws and civilization. Hence, we see primitive men all rogues. And I am sorry to say some cling with unabating tenacity to a long line of ancestors.

My countrymen pay much attention to the improvement of their stock, read long pedigrees and pay high prices for a cow. The cow is valued not for what she possesses, but for her blood. When they come to select a wife, the first inquiry is what does she possess? what is she worth? They seldom inquire whether her physical and mental abilities are suitable to them as individuals, whether the family will be on the up or the down grade. Until the union of men and women is effected with more judgment, progress in the human race must depend entirely upon education.

That our civilization can make no farther advances, is one of the great errors of the age.

Some of our customs and laws that have been in vogue since the dawn of history, can and will be set aside.

All men venerate antiquity, and to part with an old idea, or change our view of ancient justice, and venerated customs, handed down from one generation to another, through the long centuries of the past, is like burying an old friend—he is gone, but we cannot forget him.

And thus we hold on with unabating tenacity to the customs of our fathers. A man may boast of a long line of learned ancestors, and flatter himself with the idea that he was bred in a high state of civilization, while in truth he is at best only a half breed. As long as *money* elevates family, few can claim to be more than half bloods.

The laws of hereditary descent in connection with education, are the two great powers that must eventually carry the human race to the millennium.

The Jews are the most distinguished of the nations of antiquity, who established divine laws. The civil law originated with the Greeks and Romans, the gods they worshipped were a superstitious representation of the human passions, and their laws originated from the customs of the people, and were at first denominated *civil laws*, to distinguish them from the laws of other nations. Later—the term *civil law* was used to distinguish the customs and laws of the State, from the canon laws or laws of the church.

The laws called the laws of Solon and of Lycurgus, and other ancient statesmen, did not originate with these men; they only organized a code of laws founded upon the customs of the people, and suitable to the times in which they lived.

During the rise of the Roman Empire, subjugated provinces, while they were compelled to pay tribute to Rome, were still permitted to live according to their own customs, and be judged by their own laws.

After the fall of the Roman Empire, new German States were founded in the west, in which the immigrated Germans and conquered Romans lived together under the same government. The Germans had separate laws and customs of their own preserved in their new settlements, while the subdued Romans, living among them, continued to use their own laws and customs, and were judged according to them.

Hence we see the manners and customs of the people that are to be governed, lay the foundation of their laws. We should therefore adopt new manners and customs with great caution, while upon the other hand, old manners and customs that are deleterious to the well being of society, should be set aside with firmness, for as certain as the manners and customs of the dead generations have ripened into the laws of the living, the manners and customs of the living will ripen into the laws of the coming generations of men.

The common law, as recognized to-day, orignated from the manners and customs of the English people, and was at first designated the unwritten law, but we must not understand from this that the statute, or written law, did not originate in the same way, for we know that the unwritten law has ever laid the foundation of statute law in all countries.

Our laws, like our language, are gradually changing. So many new words have been engrafted on the English language, that an Englishman resurrected from the grave, where he has slept for eight hundred years, would not understand our language, or live happily under our laws. Our language is progressive, and so are our laws. Social and political customs are the blossoms of the coming law. Societies are setting aside customs which are still legal, but with the increase of numbers in society, those customs will be set aside.

The germ of a law, like a mustard seed starts from a point, and our laws to-day are half a century behind the times.

Resurrect George Washington from the grave and let him witness the flight across the continent upon the *iron horse;* let him hear the announcement of the election in New Orleans made in Washington City in twenty minutes after it is spoken by the judges, and he would think he had slept a thousand years; let him go to Mount Vernon and bring suit for possession.

> Adverse claims and the law delays,
> Would sound to him like former days.

I have said that the origin of the law is the customs of the people, and great statesmen only organize the will of the people they represent.

By this declaration it is not my design to tarnish a feather in the cap of any great man, for it is *genius* of the highest order that can fathom the bosoms of the people, that can feel with the wronged and observe the motives of the wrong-doer and apply the proper remedy. While the lamps of all past ages cast a flood of light upon the present they must reveal wrong as well as right.

To say that our laws have approached perfection, would affirm the arrival of the millennium.

The struggle of a principle in law, like the struggle of a word in a language, must depend upon its own strength.

The liberty of a people to make their laws is bounded by the line of the state; the term *United States* conveys the idea that a number of different states have united for a certain purpose. To suppose they had united for all purposes of government and law would abolish the state lines and leave but one state.

One state and a centralized government would be the inevitable fate of our country. The government has of late been to some extent revolutionized on this subject, but there are yet many questions that lie along the border line between state and federal authorities that have yet to be discussed and settled

Any law, local in its effects and republican in its form, and not in conflict with the Constitution of the United States, is a part and parcel of the liberties of the state.

You may rob me of my goods; you may rob me of my party name; but oh! God, save me from the dark demagogue who would unjustly rob me of my liberty.

The future greatness of our country depends upon the ability with which we defend the rights transmitted to us by our fathers.

When the waves of empire shall beat upon the rock of *state rights*, may some gallant son of a noble sire arise **and** proclaim thus far you may go but no farther.

In the states, like the provinces of the Great Empire

let us live under our own laws while we pay tribute to Rome.

The freedom of the Union depends upon the freedom of the states; like the character of a family depends upon the character of its individual members.

The future of our country is astounding. Revolving time will give us two hundred millions of people. The great problem of self-government has yet to be put to the test. With the accumulation of strength we accumulate the difficulties of the problem of government. Education, virtue and manhood must be increased with increasing power. Mental improvement can and ought to be offered to all classes of our people. Honest political economy in place of *political deception* should be ever held up to the view of the rising generation.

With a soil unsurpassed on the globe; throughout a broad and beautiful land; with a genius unparalleled in the history of nations; with a people brave, active and generous the future can only grow dark under the mantle of an unwise government. The public mind, like the mind of an individual, is subject to violent commotions, but in the moments of calm reflection it is more apt to appeal to reason and establish law and justice. The Romans divided the law into what they called public and private law; the latter applied to individuals, the former to the state. The law between man and man or what is properly individual, is more lasting and permanent and is seldom overthrown by revolutions in the government.

William, the conqueror, overran and revolutionized the government of England, but the Saxon inhabitants clung to their birth-right memories and the laws of Alfred the Great, and although an effort was made to change the language as well as the laws, it could not be effected, and while the blending of the Norman and Saxon tongues gave up the English language, fair-minded men to-day love the plain Saxon words.

Public law, or the administration of the government, is the great end and aim of all revolutions, and no revolution of a government in any age or country was ever accomplished without a *political party*. Revolutions are necessary; they must and will come in the order of progress; they mark, and will continue to mark, the onward march of our civilization.

But when I speak of the baneful influences of political parties, my tongue grows silently short. It would take a master of the fine arts, and require the genius of all the leading languages to guide the pen of an author, or the eloquence of an orator to draw even a faint outline of the unparalleled history of party crime.

No government can exist without a party, and while I recognize party and principle as the two great elements in political economy, I hope, and honestly trust, never to forsake principle for the sake of party.

Since the days of Grecian fables great ideas have been communicated by homely illustrations. The fable of the "Fawn and Leopard" may not be out of place here.

Near by the handsome hills of a western State, with towering tree-tops and foliage green, in wild seclusion from the haunts of men there lived a seal fat fawn. By morning's dream aroused from sleep and hungry for the new-grown grass, with nimble foot and fairy tread started out to nip the buds and breathe the morning air. Behind she left her doating dam, and wandered far away across the pleasing plain spread with carpet green and fringed with wild and wasting bloom. She brushed the dew from the growing grass and nipped the tender buds. Amid the stillness of the scene no sound was heard and she saw no fraid.

Hard by the hazel brush a leopard sat, with eager eyes and ivory teeth, half concealed, with hunger in his breast and murder in his eye; still as inaudible time to watch the coming fawn.

The scent of blood on the morning air rushed through his head and formed his feet to spring, his leap fell short, and then the frightened fawn flew with her life across the open field.

At first she ran too fast for him, 'twas down a long descent; but rising up the sloping hill, her wind grew short and faint, for want of breath, her speed lost half its force.

With iron heel and eager eyes the bloody beast approached. Thus, far away from hope or help, the fleet-footed fawn found her fate.

The fawn fitly represents principle, pure as the dew from heaven; while the leopard represents party always fond of blood.

As we enjoy our individual freedom by the union of liberty and law, we also enjoy our public freedom by the union of principle and party.

No government can exist without a party, but it must be properly blended with principle. Politicians say we must stand by our party, and they should add, we must also stand by our principles.

The United States government will eventually stereotype the ancient government of Imperial or Papal Rome. Imperial Rome, or the government of Rome under the Emperors, when they conquered a neighboring nation, permitted them to live according to their own customs, and to be judged by their own laws; while they were required to pay tribute to Rome for protection, and the Roman legions were ever ready to defend the provinces of the Empire.

Assembled under the banner of the Royal Purple, the Roman eagle was the mistress of the world.

Papal Rome, or the government of Rome under the Popes, reversed the rule when a province or State entered upon the *war path*. Rome was for sale. The State willing to surrender most of her local liberties could purchase Rome.

The fountain of power to increase the strength of party and subdue principle. Pot-house politicians are the men who would imitate Papal Rome, men who work for their party regardless of principle, men who seek the government money without rendering some service to the government, act upon the same theory of the gambler and the rogue, and ought to be classed with pot-house politicians. In this connection I remember the words of John C. Calhoun, the great political scholar of his day. Speaking of party, he said: "It is held together by the cohesive power of the public plunder." And the words of the more witty John Randolph, of Roanoke, upon the same subject: "It has seven principles, five loaves and two fishes."

In conclusion I speak to young men who have yet to come upon the stage of statesmanship; who have yet to learn the great principles of liberty and law; who have yet to stand in the council-house of this great nation; who have yet to defend the liberties of a great people; who have yet to mold the destiny of a great government. May you prove worthy of the task.

LECTURE II—TIME AND MOTION.

The back woodsman enters the forest with his ax upon his shoulder, gives the first impression made with human foot to the virgin soil; builds a log cabin; discovers the course that the waters run; gives fright to the wolf and the wild-cat, and proclaims the dominion of man. He then sinks into his grave, with no greater honor inscribed upon his banner than that of the brave pioneer.

Those who come after him erect the church and the school-house; open the roads; cultivate the ground; build towns and cities, and throw their banner to the breeze inscribed with "The Land of the Free and Home of the Brave."

Like the back-woodsman, with nature's ax on my shoulder, I venture upon untrodden ground, on the broad domain of mental philosophy; here I build my cabin; here I point out the course the waters of nature run; alarm the wolves and the wild-cats of the social circle, and open a new field in mental philosophy to those who come after me. All that I ask or expect is the honor due to a brave pioneer.

Time, thou venerable Sire and mysterious harvest hand, who gave you that old scythe that never needs the whetting stone, yet will not cut the thread of fate, or wound the gods. Is that thine only tool? thou builder of towns and cities, founder of governments and nations, and father of the arts and sciences. No mortal eye hath seen thy cradle; none shall see thy grave.

Solomon said: "There is a time to be merry and a time to be sad; a time to weep and a time to be glad." Another wise man said: "Time makes all things even;" but no philosopher has ever told us *what time is*. What is time? Time is not a thing. This book is a thing; but time is not a thing, or, in other words, time is not a cause. Time is effect, or, rather, the result of motion. We assume the position that time is not eternity, or any part of it, a proposition that is not disputed, so far as I know, by any one. We have been taught that time is a part of duration. This is a mistake. Duration is a period of time that belongs to the past, and not to the future. It applies to past ages of the world, and cannot properly be applied to ages to come; but let us establish the proposition that time is the result of motion. The earth has two motions denominated—the annual and diurnal. The earth revolves around the sun in its orbit once in three hundred and sixty-five days, and upon its axis, once in twenty-four hours. Daylight and darkness were the first divisions of time known to primitive man. There is as much night as there is day, eternally, on the earth; but, to any stationary point on the surface of the earth, day and night approaches with the rising and setting of the sun, or, in other words, day and night are the result of the motion of the earth in its diurnal revolutions, and for many ages was the only division of time known to antiquity. The first effort made by man to extend the division of time was the invention of an instrument called the sun-dial.

The first mention in the Scriptures of any instrument for keeping time is in the second book of Kings, Chap. 20, verse 11, and alludes to the dial of Ahaz, who lived and reigned at Jerusalem about 300 years after Solomon completed the temple, and about 900 years after Joshua led the Israelites over the river Jordan, about 3,400 years after Adam, the first man, according to Jewish antiquity.

Thus we see, the human race had approached the middle of the historic period before any instrument was invented for keeping time, or rather we should say, for measuring motion.

The first mention in the Scriptures made of the hour is by the prophet, Daniel, III; 6. Daniel, when a boy, was carried off from his native land in the Babylonian captivity. His book was written in Babylon, and relates to circumstances that occurred in that country. Hence we infer that the Jews obtained much of their knowledge of the sun-dial, from the Babylonians, for we are informed by Greek historians that they were the first who divided the day into twelve equal parts.

The face of the sun-dial does not differ materially from the face of the clock of the present day. While the hand of the clock is but an artificial shadow to point out the time or rather to indicate the progress of the *Earth* in its *revolution* upon its *axis*, the motion of the clock must correspond precisely with the motion of the *Earth* or the clock will not keep *correct time*.

Clocks to run with cog-wheels were first invented in France in the year 996. Clocks to run with a pendulum were not invented until 1630; and there is not a *dictionary* or *lexicon* that has ever been *published* in the *world* that gives a true definition of the word *time*.

Stand with your face toward the east at twilight and observe the heavenly harnessed team of day peep over the eastern hills at you, then start like a sky-rocket through the atmosphere west, at the rate of one thousand miles an hour, and you will see the glorious god of day peeping over the eastern hills at you forever.

Now suppose, for the sake of the argument, that you have a good watch in your pocket, a true time-piece, as we say, and that you could elevate yourself just above the highest peak of the mountain top and remain still—*the sun is still and you are still—your watch is right and the sun is right.*

The surface of the earth would pass you at the rate of one thousand miles an hour. If you were elevated at sunrise the sun would be rising all the time; if at noon it would be noon all the time; if at sunset it would be sunset all the time —so far as your observation would be concerned.

Now let us suppose that you left a white flag on the *Earth* where you were *elevated*, and that you were elevated at 6 o'clock, when the flag comes around again you look at your watch and it indicates six o'clock. The flag would be your only evidence that your watch was right, and was *measuring motion*. We call the result of that measure *time*.

To realize *day* and *night* we must be confined to a local spot on the surface of the *Earth*. The light of day bursts upon the people of New York before it arouses the sleepers of California, and the shades of night gather 'round the people of New York before the sun sinks in the Pacific to the eyes of California.

But why should I continue on this part of the subject? Learned and wise men everywhere agree that motion measures time, for there is no evading the *evidence*; it is a proposition that proves itself. But they say that motion does not produce *time*. I confess that motion does not produce *eternity* but contend that it does produce *time*.

Here then is the tug of war.

We find ourselves a lonely traveler in a strange land, weary, tired and hungry. Yonder is a cottage, let us apply for food and rest. We stand before the gate and inform the monarch of the premises that we are tired and hungry. He orders a sheep driven out of his lot, and pointing at it with his index finger says, if you don't eat that sheep, *head* and *horns, you are not hungry.*

More than forty years ago, after having been raised in a

corn field, I came upon the stage of action, with a diploma from a log *school house* in the backwoods of Kentucky, *hungry* and *thirsty* for information, and with the elastic palate of a hopeful student swallowed everything—*head and horns.*

To get rid of the *horns,* I emancipated myself from the tyranny of the *schools,* and appealed to the original copy—which is *nature.*

Now it is a self-evident proposition that motion cannot accomplish anything without the direction of *intellect.*

Then *motion* does not *measure time* but *intellect measures motion,* and we call the result of that measure *time.*

Measuring time reminds me of the report made by a man who *attempted to measure the imagination.* He said: "It is as large as the *globe* and smaller than a *mustard seed*—it fills the *whole universe* and you can get it in a *thimble*—it exists throughout all *space* and has no *existence*—it will make you as rich as a *bond-holder*—with *it* you can fill all your fields with *cattle,* and make a two-year old colt in a *minute.*"

Measure time; a moment, half a moment, here, fleeting, gone forever. What is time before it is measured? or what is time measured out of? You can measure a piece of cloth because that is a thing; you can measure a large pile of wheat with a small cup, but you will measure the wheat all up. So likewise, if time was measured out of duration, duration would all be measured up; and if out of eternity, eternity would all be measured up. To say time is measured out of time is absurd and ridiculous nonsense. Motion no more measures time than the waves on the sea measure the water; the wave is the result of the wind, when the wind lulls and becomes still the ocean becomes calm—the wave has sunk. Time is the result of the motion of the earth; when the earth becomes still (if it ever does) the wave of our time will be *lost* and sink in the ocean of *eternity.* Hence we see the force that was in the language of the English poet when he said—

> The bless'd to-day, is as completely so,
> As who began a thousand years ago."

A year of time is determined by the motion of a planet around the sun in its orbit, consequently every planet has a different year of *time*, and just in proportion as they differ in their speed of motion and distance from the sun. The *exact time* of the earth's motion around the sun in its orbit was not *ascertained* for many ages. In the morning of the historic period, when every man was his own astronomer, the rising and setting of the *dog star*, as it was called, was observed with no ordinary interest. The ancient Thebans, who first cultivated *astronomy* in Egypt, determined the length of the year by the number of its risings. The Egyptians watched it with mingled apprehensions of hope and fear; it foretold the rising of the river Nile and admonished them to sow their fields. Julius Cæsar came very near regulating the *calendar*, but the astronomers in his day, in their observations of the earth in its orbit, made an error of eight minutes and forty-eight seconds, and it was found in 1582 that in the run of 1648 years the true time was ten days ahead of the recorded time, and in order to reach the true time without disturbing the records of all Christendom, the Pope of Rome issued a proclamation, or bull, calling the 5th day of October the 15th. And this is the origin of old and new style of time. You have all heard of *old Christmas*, when the cows kneel at midnight, the chickens crow, and the dogs bark. The new style of time was not adopted in England until 1752—one hundred and seventy years after the correction—in the reign of George II.

The revolution of the earth around the sun in its orbit determines a year of time and always did, though it required many ages to ascertain that fact. While the earth passes around the sun in its orbit once, it revolves upon its axis 366 times and only produces 365 days. And this brings us to consider solar and siderial time or solar and siderial motion.

We can best represent it by the hands of a clock. You must remember that the motion of the earth in its orbit and upon its axis are both in the same direction. The earth rises up from the west, so to speak, and turns to the east in its diurnal revolutions, causing the approach of day and night to every local spot upon its surface. The motion of the earth in its orbit is also from west to east, rising up, so to speak, ninety-five millions of miles above the sun, and sinking the same distance below the sun.

The orbit of the earth is perpendicular, and not horizontal, as up and down, appear to our senses. Now let us call the motion or speed of the hour hand the earth's orbit, and the motion of the minute hand the earth's axis. We now place both hands at twelve o'clock, and say that it is noon, or the sun is on the meridian. When the minute hand passes round and comes again to the figure 12, the earth has accomplished one revolution upon its axis; but the earth has also moved one degree in the same direction, as represented by the hour hand, consequently the earth must move one degree further to overtake the hour hand and bring the sun on the meridian again. This distance is divided into 365 degrees. One is lost every day, consequently in 366 revolutions of the earth upon its axis we realize only 365 days, and this is solar and siderial time, or solar and siderial motion.

There is another illustration of this problem. Let three men agree that one shall start around the earth, traveling east, and that one shall make the same journey, traveling west, and the third shall remain at the place of starting. Each man shall keep a correct tally of every day that transpires in a year, by cutting a notch on a stick. At the end of the year the two travelers return, having traversed the globe, and compare notes. The one who remained stationary will have 365 notches; the one who traveled east will have 364 notches; the one who traveled west will have 366 notches. Now, if these men were measuring or keeping time, they would agree. The fact is, they have measured *motion* and have not measured *time*. One traveled with the motion of the earth, and maintained solar time; the other traveled against the motion of the earth, and gained one day.

A month or a week is an artificial division of time, adopted for convenience. Seven days have been called a week from the remotest antiquity of the Jews. Prior to the reign of Numa Pompilius, the second King of Rome, the year was divided into ten months, or thirteen moons.

The motion of the earth produces the time of the earth, or what we recognize as our time; for every planet has its own motion, and consequently its own time.

When the earth ceases to move (if it ever does), our time will also cease; but the time on the other planets will not cease, if they continue in their motion. We can compare their motions with the motions of the earth, and note the difference in their time and our time.

If the earth was bursted to make moons for some other planet, we have no evidence that the motion of the other planets would be changed or altered, and as long as they maintain their motion they will maintain their time.

The planet Venus revolves upon her axis once in 23 hours, 21 minutes, and 7 seconds, consequently her day is about twenty-five minutes shorter than ours. She passes around the sun in her orbit in seven and a half months of our time. While the earth measures two years, Venus deals out three years and forty-five days to her inhabitants.

The planet Mars is the bright star that we saw in the east in September and October, a little after sunset. He revolves upon his axis in 24 hours, 37 minutes, and 23 seconds, consequently his day is about forty-two minutes longer than ours. He passes around the sun in his orbit in twenty-two and a half months of our time, consequently it takes nearly two of our years to make one for the planet Mars.

Those two planets are next to the earth—Venus on the inside and Mars on the outside track.

But let us go 'way yonder near the edge of the solar system, and observe the planet Jupiter He revolves upon his axis in 9 hours, 55 minutes, and 50 seconds, consequently he crowds two of his days into one of ours, and has about four hours left. He stands boldly out from the sun a distance of 495 millions of miles—400 millions of miles further from the sun than the earth is—and he moves around the sun in his orbit in a little less than twelve of our years, consequently while a boy of his inhabitance is arriving at twelve years of age, one of our boys would become a venerable sire of one hundred and forty-four years.

Now let us visit all of the planets we have named, and take the watch with us. When we arrive on the velvet shores of Venus we will move the regulator of the watch—the spring that regulates the motion of the watch—so it will run twenty-five minutes fast in a day, and when we meet the Monarch of that planet we can tell him the time of day—because our watch is brought precisely to the motion of his planet, or world.

When we arrive on the bloody shores of the planet Mars we will deaden the main spring of the watch, so it will run forty-two minutes slow in a day, and we will have the time or measure of the motion of that planet.

But when we arrive on the distant shores of Jupiter what can we do with the watch? We will have to double the power of the main spring of our watch to keep the time or measure the motion of that planet—because he revolves on his axis *twice* while the earth revolves *once*, and has about four hours left.

Does not these illustrations make it clear that clocks and watches measure motion?

What, then, is time? The result of motion; or, in other words, motion produces time, but does not produce eternity.

What then is duration? As I said before, duration is a period of time that belongs to the past. Mark what I say— for all of the wise men of the past, from Numa Pompilius to the Pope of Rome—all learned authorities, both sacred and profane—have said that time is a part of duration. They put the cart before the horse—duration is a part of time, and belongs to the past. It is a law of nature that effect cannot precede cause; no man can build a house before he prepares the materials. Duration is the sum of motion, and cannot exist before that motion is performed. Rome was founded 750 years before the Christian era; that is, the earth accomplished 750 revolutions around the sun in its orbit from the founding of Rome until the inauguration of Christianity. That 750 years is a period of time, or a part of time, that we call duration, and belongs to the past. 1100 years transpired— that is, the earth made 1100 revolutions around the sun in its orbit from the time Solomon built the temple at Jerusalem until the birth of Christ. And, according to the most approved system of archæology, 5440 years transpired—that is, the earth made 5440 revolutions around the sun, from the creation by Moses until the meek and lowly Jesus preached His Gospel on the mount in Palestine

All of those are periods of duration recorded on the page of history. But if you wish a more extended idea of duration, go back with me behind the historic period—go back a hundred thousand years—go back a hundred thousand centuries—go back a hundred million of centuries—go back until the mind turns upon itself, and there is an idea not yet expressed—*eternity*. Turn the imagination loose, and go forward, but remember, duration does not express the idea, anticipation is before, duration is behind—*time* has disappeared.

Observe the intellect, solitary and alone, in the broad field of space. Space, by affinity, is eternity—an open field without end—a fit home, for eternity can not dwell in a local spot. Time and motion belong to the planets. The planets belong to space. The forecast of intellect, may realize eternity—and here we pause, on the distant border of human thought, for we come not here again until the close of our last lecture. Getting down upon the ground-work of nature and her laws, I come to speak of *Motion*.

Motion, is a principle. I hold my hand here, and move it there. My hand is a thing, but the change of its position is a principle—motion—and it is the first principle of nature. The whole universe is in motion. The sun is still to his planets, but the sun, together with his planets, are moving through the broad field of space around an unknown center. The flowers of the field, the majestic oak, the vegetable, and all of the animal kingdom, could not be developed without the principle of motion. Our broad and beautiful fields that wave with golden heads on the days of harvest—our towns, villages and cities, and the iron horse that consolidates them into one city—together with all the works of nature and of art. The broad and placid river, that bears the products of our labor on its bosom, as it rolls on in its majesty to the ocean, and the river itself, is the result of the principle of motion.

Water, in small and minute particles, traverses the atmosphere, condensing, it falls to the ground in drops of rain, and fills up the rivulets, that wind their wandering way across the valleys, and fill up the rivers, and the rivers traversing a continent, return to the ocean. Not only on this continent, but also the continents of Europe, Africa and Asia—

not only on the continents of earth, but on all the planets that belong to the solar system, and all of these streams of water are produced by the heat of the sun, but the heat of sun does not produce the water So, likewise, the fleeting moments of time, fill up the minutes, the minutes fill up the hours, the hours fill up the days, the days fill up the years, the years fill up the centuries, and the centuries roll on in their majesty, to the ages, not only upon earth, but on all the planets that belong to the solar system. And all of these streams of time are produced by motion. But motion does not produce the universe. By the term universe, we do not allude alone to the solar system, but to the broad expanse of the unfolded heavens. The ancients had a very obscure idea of the heavens. The telescope was invented in 1588, and improved by Galileo, who was compelled by a superstitious court, on the 28th day of June, 1633, at the peril of his life, to deny with his lips the great facts that science and nature had unfolded to his truthful heart.

Go with me to the telescope, on a clear night, when the pulse of all pre-conceived ideas is still; observe the one hundred million of fixed stars—they are called fixed because they are so remote from the earth, that the orbit of the earth, one hundred and ninety millions of miles, produces no perceptible change in their locality. They are supposed to be suns as large as ours, with planets revolving 'round them. And on those planets are rivers as long as the Missouri, and broad as the Amazon, and mountains and valleys, filled with life and motion. Go on in the imagination beyond the utmost limits of telescopic vision, and we are lost in wonder. Every spark of light is a world. God is everywhere. When this glorious revelation is unfolded to our view, we are less concerned with the philosophy of creation, than we are in asking ourselves the question: Will man sleep in the grave for ever? This question will be more fully answered at the close of our lectures, but for the satisfaction of the impatient, we answer, no. It is contrary to all nature, and to everything that we see made manifest around us, to suppose that the mind perishes like the body. Nature is always true to herself. An organ of the human brain, has painted a great castle, in which there is every delight to entertain, amuse and instruct the intellect, where there is no pain, no sorrow and no weeping; where the aisles and the walks stretch a-w-a-y y-o-n-d-e-r beyond the remotest conception of the human brain; where pleasure flows in upon the travelers from innumerable avenues on every foot of the way; where departed friends who have been made dear to the heart by the warmest ties of affection, are met again. But the castle is elevated, and we have no ladder to reach it. Oh! wretched man that I am, who shall deliver me from this dead body?

We shall, in the course of these lectures, endeavor to unfold the beautiful principles of nature. But for the present we must return to the philosophy of motion. We have spoken of the motion of the universe, we must now speak of motion with regard to man. The field is broad and full of beautiful illustrations. We only call your attention to one. It is one that reflects many others. I take hold of anything with my right hand and throw it 'round with more ease than I do with my left hand, and why? Because the principle of motion has been more thoroughly applied to my right, than it has to my left hand. And this principle holds good throughout all nature.

Take two little boys, of equal endowment and physical strength. (Your arms are equal in infancy.) Educate one of them, as you educate the right hand, and educate the other, as you educate the left hand. When they arrive to manhood there will be the same difference between them, that there is between the right and the left hand, and from the same cause, and this principle holds good mentally as well as physically.

The first and great principle of nature, is motion, action, industry. There is no greatness attainable in any calling without it, either *physically* or *mentally*. Great men in all ages, and among all nations, have worked their way up from the bottom. Like a seed cast upon the earth, to rise up and unfold the branches, the blossoms, and the fruit, whose tender buds are first directed by the delicate hand of a faithful mother.

Henry Clay, the great American *statesman*, was once a mill boy, and rode an old blind horse through the swamps of his native State, on a bag of meal. The gentle breeze that rustled through the infant locks, clustering beneath a home-made cap, may have whispered in a still small voice the living principle of *motion*. Without fame and without fortune, but with industry and integrity, he winged a golden way from the swamps of his native State, to the mountain-top of fame in the United States.

If there be in this assembly, any little boy upon whom fortune has frowned, I mean as to money; to him I say, go to work mentally, preserve the body and the brain from all demoralizing influences, ponder over the experience of past ages by the midnight lamp, and as certain as the sun rises in the future you will *meet your reward*.

If you have no mother, and those to whom you are amenable are neglecting your character, go to work, and build up your own character, lay the foundation stones deep in the ground, run the walls up plumb and true, let every part of the edifice meet the eye of the beholder in harmony, and you will become a great man.

Julius Cæsar has been dead 1922 years, imperishable fame is stamped on his name; with no counseler but ambition, and no friend but his sword, he crossed the Rubicon and laid the foundation of the *Roman Empire* If you have no desire to become Cæsar, and wish to make a dog of yourself, go sleep in the barn, lay 'round the premises, and scratch fleas, feed on the crumbs thrown out at the door, and the first thing you know, you will begin to bark.

One more word to doubtful men, and I conclude. If there be in this assembly any one who feels aggrieved at this discourse, because it contains more philosophy than it does religion, to them I say, the bones of my ancestors for six generations, sleep beneath the green sod in the church-yards of my native land. They filled their cups from the measure of faith offered up in their day. It would not become a brave manhood, to throw a spot of tarnish on their memory, or leave their tombs for the home of the bat and the owl. For all that I am, and all that I hope to be, in this life, or in the life to come, is justly due to early impressions, made upon a youthful brain by a christian mother.

LECTURE III.—MIND AND ORGANISM.

Nothing that is not solid, true and refined—dare ask public audience of mankind.

Mental philosophy has engaged the attention of the wise men of the world, in all ages, and among all nations. Zoroaster among the Persians, Plato among the Greeks, and St. Paul among the Jews, left impressions behind them on the subject of *mental philosophy*, that will last as long as the brain will think, or stamp a thought in *marble* transmitted to posterity. When we look back upon primitive man, we see him destitute of the *arts* and *sciences*, rude, and barbarous to his own *species*. And when we observe the centuries rolling on, turning up at each revolution some new discovery and unfolding principles that contribute to the comfort of man, physically and mentally, the question naturally presents itself to us, Why do men become wiser? What is it, that illuminates the path-way of every art and of every science? What is the motive power impelling the onward march of our civilization? Who has ever unfolded the dominion of *mind* over *matter?*

That mind or intellect is in the universe, no one will dispute. But how produced, and how sustained, is the question. We proceed upon the theory, that the brain is the seat, of head-quarters of the mind. Does the mind originate in the brain, or is it external?

I shall offer you some *startling evidences* that mind is external, a principle or element prevading the universe, and this is a *new departure* from the great cardinal principles laid down by the old philosophers.

We live in a *progressive age*, while every art and every science has advanced with wonderful rapidity, mental philosophy has been left to slumber in the tomb of the dark ages.

But let us proceed with the evidence, sustaining the proposition, that mind is external.

The variegated colors of the rainbow, the view of the heavens and of the earth, together with all the visible beauties of nature, are introduced to the brain by external means, for the eye is but the window of the brain; and as the rays of the light of the sun, reveal and display all of the visible beauties of the universe, so also, the rays of the great star of intellect, reveal and display all of the beauties of *wisdom*.

When we are in a dark room, we see dimly; when we come out to the light, we see plainly. In our native ignorance, we are mentally blind, whether it be the childhood of a nation, or an individual; when we are brought out to the light of experience by the institutions of our predecessors, we see plainly many things that we did not see in our native ignorance. If you say that equal instruction should equally enlighten all men, I answer, it would, if all men were endowed with the same mental glass, but this is not the case, for while some are endowed with a mental glass thin and transparent, others are thick, cast in the dark, so dead and opaque in themselves, that the concentrated rays of the great star of intellect would not penetrate them in forty years. The eyes, the ears, the nose, the tongue and the nerves of the body, are all external and visible organs of the brain, by which information is received.

No man can see with his ears or hear with his eyes, can love whom he hates or hate whom he loves, and when he is mentally deaf to the notes of music, it is no evidence that he is mentally deaf to the voice of love; and every organ of the brain performs its office precisely in proportion to its capacity. A man with good eyes sees well, with good ears hears well, and this brings us to consider upon the internal and invisible organs of the brain.

The organ of music is more plainly and better developed in some races of men than it is in others, and in some individuals of the same race than in others. The organs of self-esteem, combativeness, hope, the love of home, and many others, are more fully developed in some individuals than in others. All men do not see alike, pride alike, love alike, or stay at home alike. In accordance with the organism of the brain do they act. We conclude, therefore, that the brain is a set of organs animated by a principle or element pervading the universe.

Let us make an effort to identify the *internal* with the *external* organs of the brain. We will do so by asking a supposed individual a few plain questions. Why did you not see the procession that came to town this morning? Because my eyes have been put out. Why did you not hear the rolling of the wheels and the tramp of the horses? Because my ears have failed; I am deaf. Why did you not smell that remarkable odor that accompanied the train? Because my nose is stopped up; I have a dreadful cold.

Let us restore the external mental organs and continue the questions. Why did you not imitate the beautiful music that was in the procession? Because I cannot sing; I have no ear for music. Why did you not draw a pencil picture of the train? Because I have no mechanism, no talent for drawing. Why did you not stand erect and show yourself to the best advantage while the train was passing? Because I have no self-esteem. But, an objector says, that is phrenology, and no proof that mind is external. I answer—It identifies mental organism.

We will now proceed with another class of evidences

that makes it clear that mind is a living principle pervading the universe. Observe that industrious mechanic. He is up early and bright in the morning, full of hope and action, determined to earn an honest living for himself and family. His eyes behold all the beauties of nature, his ears note every sound of his hammer, his genius or mechanism trace every line of his pencil. His days work is over; he faithfully returns to his domicile; the last scene of the day closes upon our observation. His garments are laid aside; stretched upon his couch he closes his eyes, shutting out the light of the world; the busy bustle of the day is over and the pulse of the town is still, all the nerves of his body have ceased to vibrate; the organs of his brain are all closed; he is held in the sweet embrace of nature's soft nurse; the man is asleep; his mind is gone; intellect does not sleep; it is organism; every organ in the brain closes up like the eye, and this is the lethargy we call sleep—death's half brother.

When there is no concert of action or harmony with the brain organs in closing up, when they are all closed, except the organs of memory and fancy or imagination, we realize what we call restless sleep, disturbed sleep, the sleep of mesmerism, somnambulism, and all other kinds of sleep that produce wonderful dreams to delight and afflict humanity.

Do not understand us to say that our brain organs are all in action when we are awake, for this would be an error. Few persons can laugh and cry at the same time. No man can be in a good humor and angry at the same time. Asleep or awake we do one thing at a time. Persons sometimes walk and handle things in their sleep, but when the organ of time is brought into action we are awake.

Now let us put the proposition that the mind is external to another test. Let us take a man that you have all known for many years to be an honest man and a good citizen. He has met with a sad misfortune; lost his pocket-book; close the door and let us detect the thief. Hold! I made a mistake in regard to the article. He has lost his *mind*. Where shall we go to look for it and how can we describe it? Let us take him to the lunatic asylum; the doctors will apply soothing remedies to his brain, and if they succeed in restoring a healthy action to his mental organs they will find his mind. But where will they find it? They will find it ready to enter his brain as soon as good health to organism is restored. They will find it where the sleeping man finds it when he awakes; they will find that it is an element pervading the universe.

Our mental organs are subject to disease; we go blind, deaf, or crazy. Sometimes the eye is affected, and we see two objects where there is but one. When the eye is restored we see nature as it is. Every organ in the brain may thus be disturbed, until a man will not see nature in a natural way. To him friends are enemies, love is hatred, reason is fiction, and affection worthless; he is crazy. Sometimes one of the internal and invisible organs of the brain is afflicted and diseased, while the others are not. We have a monomaniac.

There is a case recorded in history of a wealthy man who was said to be crazy. The accusation was brought by his brother, and it was supposed that the brother wished to get possession of his property. The case was taken into court; the learned attorneys questioned him for more than an hour without getting the slightest evidence of insanity. The judge and a crowded court room were almost ready to declare the man sane, when some one whispered in the ear of the plaintiff, "Ask him about religion." The moment the question was put he rose to his feet and exclaimed, "*I am the Christ!*" He was insane on the subject of religion; upon all other subjects perfectly rational.

A man may be blind, but while he is blind it is no evidence that he is deaf. The open and visible organs of the brain are manifest to all men. The invisible mental organs are only revealed by the deepest research. The case of the monomaniac stands before you as one of my witnesses. Cross-examine him, dissect his mind, otherwise, if you can.

Careful reflection upon the subject of mental philosophy opens every man's eyes. The light of the sun will not illuminate the brain if you shut your eyes. And the light of the great star of intellect will not illuminate the brain if you shut the eyes of your mental organs, permit them to remain closed, or become diseased. When the eyes grow dim we put on glasses, when self esteem is low we put on a new coat and feel prouder, when we disagree in philosophy we should put on the mantle of charity.

We will now call your attention to the last case in this class of evidences.

The mind can be expelled from the brain by a chemical operation, and therefore must be external. Let us take another sensible man, whom we all know to be a sensible man in every sense of the word manhood, give him a gill of whisky and a chemical operation commences in his stomach, repeat the dose and the chemicals begin to simmer, repeat again, and again and they begin to boil; the man is drunk; not only drunk, he is also a fool. His mind has been expelled from his brain—steam occupies its place. Cool down the steam with ice water and buttermilk, get the man sober, and his mind returns. Oh! God, is not that a noble principle hovering 'round a wretched man; while his body is wallowing in the mud; as soon as he can raise his head and wipe the mud from his brow, deserted reason, insulted and abused, without warrant or authority, kindly re-enters the brain.

If there be in this assembly any who feel aggrieved at this description of a drunken man, to them I say, it is with no feelings of animosity against the man, for the man has been driven out of the body, and it is the body that is drunk and degraded.

Many years ago, before the days of the red ribbon, I lived in a southern village. In the dusk of the evening I saw a man, or rather the *body* of a man, fall upon the sidewalk. With two other friends we approached that body; we met the steam of whisky; not dead, but drunk. We carried that body into a back-room and laid it on a bed. The face indicated the Caucasian race, the costume respectability, nothing more did that body reveal. There was no *mind there; no man there;* to us that body was a stranger. We all turned in and slept through the night. Who do you suppose came early next morning and claimed that body. Bill Jones, a man who lived at a distance, and whom we all knew by reputation, for Bill was a public man. We preserved the body, God preserved the mind, and when the mind came back Bill Jones came with it.

We now leave Bill Jones and return to the subject of all subjects. The foundation *stone* and *bed rock* of all philosophy is *intellect*.

I do not claim the ability to unfold *all* the beauties of *intellect*. I feel like a stranger in a woodland country, only blazing a pathway that may be worked out into a highway by some more learned and illustrious mind, who may this night, couched in infant garb, be slumbering in some log cabin, somewhere in the broad domain of our beautiful land, or way forward in the future womb of time, to come upon the stage of action when I have mingled with the worthless trash of time, *to forget and be forgotten.*

We live in a great country, our people are awakening from a long night of ignorance. The *modus operandi* of mental improvement is just beginning to emerge above the eastern horizon of our civilization. We who live to-day are only standing in the twilight of the great star of intellect, that will illuminate like a noon-day sun all coming generations of men.

Sleep on, sweet babe—the gentle influences of *mind* will gradually arouse thy torpid brain. The infant brain is like a casket with blank pages, which is to be closely printed, and positively stereotyped by eternal circumstances.

Let us go to that fond American mother and take her little son, nine months old. We will not take the child ruthlessly from the mother's arms, but let us take him for the sake of the argument. Transport him across the water, place him in a French family; the French woman will be as kind to him as his own mother; raise him up in all the beauties of manhood. But he will speak the French language and not understand a word of the language of his mother tongue. So, likewise if you take the infant of a French lady and give it to an American woman, it will speak the English language. And if you would take the infant of a Christian mother and give it to the better-half of a cut-throat, far removed from good society, in some dark retreat, struggling for existence by robbery and theft, I care not how kind the adopted parents of that child may be (in their way) when he grows up to manhood, he will be a cut-throat and a robber. And if a Christian woman go like guardian angel into this dark retreat, and take an infant born to those people, transport it across the gulf, that will separate it from its nativity, surround it with good society, and raise it up in a Christian family, that boy will become a good citizen and an honest man.

These are general rules, from which there is no appeal except to the laws of hereditary descent, of which we intend to speak. Would to God, that I could indelibly impress these facts upon the brain of every mother in America.

Teach your children the bright lessons of temperance, virtue, truth and honesty; stamp them on the infant brain, and you will elevate the manhood of your country. No great man ever had a common mother. God's blessing is upon the mother of every bright little boy if she will heed the voice of nature. Do not talk to your little son like he was a puppy; talk to him like you would to a man, and you will cultivate his manhood to rise up in a tower of strength, and vindicate the memory of his mother.

And let me say to every mother in this assembly, if you are oppressed by hard-favored-fortune, and see others around you enjoying things you can not have, be not discouraged. Remember that your intellect is the storehouse of your children. There must they go for the precious jewels of distinction that will shine upon the garments of their character, in the crowded highways of the world. There must they go for the oil to illuminate their pathway through the darkest deserts of the land. Turn them not away with empty hands, and when the last scene has closed upon their eyes, and the last word is spoken by the lips, that word will be God and my mother.

The infant loves the brightest light, with what unabating tenacity it will gaze at the burning lamp. The eye is a mental organ, and all of our mental organs love the brightest lights. When the light of evil is held up in brilliant colors the young mind is attracted in that direction. Oh! how many mothers we see who are so engaged with household work that the little child is given up to the care of a wicked and ignorant nurse. The force of education is acknowledged by all parties yet but few seem to observe the early period of its commencement.

When we have no eyes, we do not recognize the light of the sun, though the whole universe is filled with light. And if we fail to be just, virtuous, and happy, it is not because there is no justice, virtue, and happiness, it is because we have no mental organs to receive the impressions; it is because we have not cultivated these organs.

Some say that this philosophy destroys moral accountability. To them I answer: If every father in the land would refuse to lend the aid of his strong arms, to anything that produces evil, and every mother in the land would stamp upon the infant brain of her children, the bright lessons of virtue, truth and honesty, for three generations, the *Devil* would have to camp out, for he would not find entertainment in the humblest cottage in the land.

One generation works for the benefit of the next. How many fathers toil through sunshine and storm, for half a century, to lay up a store of *gold* for their children, and send them out into the broad world with full pockets and *empty heads*. How many mothers labor from the dawn of day until the dusk of evening, brushing the dust from her chambers and darkening up her rooms, that no bright ray of light may approach her infant, in its cradle.

Oh! mistaken mother, hear a lesson from the Mammoth Cave, in Kentucky; in that cave there is a river, in that river there is fish, *and those fish have no eyes*. No bright ray of light ever goes to that river and the eye of the fish not being illuminated, disappears.

Oh! *how cruel!* to shut up a little prattling babe in a dark place. Throw it around loose, if you wish the windows of its brain, and looking-glass of its soul, to beam with beauty.

One generation lives for another *mentally* as well as *physically*. We should all remember that for all that we are, as good men and women, we are indebted to our parents, and the society in which we were reared.

Now let us suppose, for the sake of the argument, that we perform all kinds of misdeeds, and practice all kinds of evil, for any considerable length of time. With this example before our children the race would go back to barbarism.

Old men are passing away. This great country with its lakes and its rivers, towns and cities, government and destiny, will soon be transmitted to the hands of our children : many of whom are now in the blossom of infancy, and *arms* of their mothers.

There is no patriotism in all the wide world, that equals true love of children. He who has no sympathy for the children, and will do nothing for the benefit of posterity, is no friend of his country. He is wandering in doubt and darkness, no bright ray of light from the great star of intellect has ever penetrated the dark recesses of his brain.

Whenever I see (if I shall live to see), the great minds of the country, taking hold of *evil* by the horns, and removing the bulls of error out of the pale of society, and leading our children to the fountains of nature, baptizing them in the water of progress, I will feel like St. John when he said : " I saw an angel come down from heaven ; having the key of the bottomless pit, and a great chain in his hand, and he laid hold of the dragon—that old serpent—which is the *Devil* and *Satan*, and bound him a thousand years.'

It is an easy going hobby-horse to charge the short-comings of humanity to the *Devil*. Society molds the character of her children. When a good mold is cast—the *Devil*—is cast out. Society molds the minds of our youth, this fact all parents feel—they may deny it with the lips. But let the villainous face of vice approach the sacred nursery of their children, and they will confess it with the truthful heart.

If you want morality, you must cultivate it in the infant brain, not in a few isolated cases but throughout the broad neighborhood. You had as well plant corn without turning the hogs out of the field, as raise your children surrounded with the sinks of corruption.

How many, in our towns and cities, have parlors shut up with thousands for the moth to eat. Go to them with the common school tax, and they think the *Devil* is after 'em with a *sharp stick*.

When a new idea comes upon the stage, it comes as a stranger. And if its mission be to a crowd the old idea off the stage, there is a herculean task before it. The old idea, though it may be false philosophy, has its old friends and associates. Everybody knows it and everybody is ready to assist it. The new idea must fight single-handed and alone. Thus we see in all ages of the world, new ideas have appeared and sunk again, to remain in the dark for ages.

When Galileo told the people that the earth moved, the old idea that the earth was the center of the universe, backed by a host of friends, crowded the new idea off the stage, to slumber in darkness until it was resurrected by Sir Isaac Newton.

I come now to speak of mind more in detail, and of its power on the mental organs. Thought is the result of action, the action of anything is the result of power. The running boy, or the walking man, whose steps are directed by the mind, is slow to realize that fact, because some of the operations of the mind are so refined, that they are almost imperceptible. When asleep or dead we do not walk or run.

There is a living power and a mental power, mysteriously blended in the elements of nature. No silent brain ever thinks, while in that condition. Hence the sleeping man does not think, yet he does live. And upon this mysterious separation of the mental and the living power, we conclude that life developes organism, and the mental element operating upon the brain organs produces *sensation*, which is the dividing link between the vegetable and animal kingdom, and the ground-work of the mental light of the world. That life developes organism without producing sensation, thought or mind, is a fact known to all physicians, and to every student of nature.

Life and mind are two parallel powers, running in the same direction, and apparently working with the same tools.

Life builds the house, mind occupies it, that is its residence is in the mental organs. The body may become diseased, broken down, the tenement so shattered, that life is almost extinct; while the mind remains romantic and bright as the morning star. On the other hand the body may remain firm and bucksome, as a blue-head buffalo, and the mind dwindle into a narrow channel, as dark as the valley of death, and gloomy as the image of night.

The character of all our sensations is produced by the mental organ, brought into action. The sound of a bell produces a sensation on the brain, through a mental organ—*the ear.*

Form, shape and beauty produce a sensation on the brain, through a mental organ, the eye.

The mental element passing through the organ of combativeness produces a sensation on the brain, but it is not a sensation of love, and when the mental element passes through the organ of love it will not produce a sensation of hatred.

The crowded streets of a commercial city produce a sensation on the brain, but it is not a sensation of solitude.

Go with me to the deep confines of a distant valley, where no trace of human foot is found. The wild flowers unfold their beauty by the side of the brook. The vine clings to the branch of the majestic oak with unabating tenacity. The blue arch of heaven terminates the vision and a sensation is produced on the brain. It is solitude, admiration and awe.

All of our sensations are received through the mental organs, and where there is no brain organ for any given sensation, passion or feeling, that feeling cannot be produced.

But the old philosophers say mind is internal, produced by the brain, and power of life, *and here we lock horns.* We have stripped this old philosophy of its overcoat. Now let us take its undergarments, not with a graceless grasp, but with the tender fingers of nature's soft hand.

The old philosophers say life produces brain and brain produces mind inseparably and indistinct. Ocular demonstration compels them to admit that mind is sometimes absent from the brain while life is not. In this case life ceases to produce mind. How is this? What checks the thought of a sleeping man? Let every one in this assembly stop thinking. *Stop*. Don't think about anything. It is impossible, yet when you sleep your thought stops.

The old philosophers say when you sleep the engineer shuts off steam. This engineer incognito in the waking state has had different names in different ages of the world. He is now usually called FREE WILL. He is a good engineer, but not always on duty. He sometimes permits the fireman to usurp his office. This fireman has also had different names in different ages of the world. He is now called Old Nick.* He is a good fireman but a bad engineer. His object is to run off the track. He would have been discharged long ago, but he keeps up the sham.

Free will is constantly admonished to watch Old Nick, for they say that when the grave station is passed, if Old Nick is not subdued, he'll kick free will overboard and run the thing off the track.

Personifying the passions or mental organs is one of the relics of the dark ages.

The Greeks and Romans were the first phrenologists in the world. They predicated upon the organ of combativeness the existence of God Mars, who delighted in the blood and carnage of the battle field.

They placed a bandage over the eyes of Cupid to establish the axiom that love hides a multitude of faults. No wonder the Hebrew prophet exclaimed, man is strange and wonderfully made.

---
* The Devil.

As I said before when a man sleeps his brain organs all close up like the eye. When he awakes the light illuminates his brain through the eye and the mental element illuminates his brain through the brain organs, and he is immediately under the influence of his will? *Not so*, but of experience and desire. Experience is the light of the past, desire the gratification of the passions.

Do not understand me to say a man has no will, for that would be an error. I say his will is formed or brought into being by predominating passions. It may be half white, but it is not free born.

Experience teaches us that honey is sweet and the bee will sting. If the sensation of appetite is stronger than the sensation of fear we will take the honey.

We see the way before us. The sensations of vice invite us on, while the sensations of virtue hold us back.

A struggle of sensations here ensues that is forcibly described by St. Paul : "The good that I would I do not, but the evil that I would not that I do."

We find ourselves under the influence of mental feelings. Our best and only true guide is experience. Holy men of old said, the way of the transgressor is hard. Disease, disgrace, darkness and death lie before him. Experience invites him to return to the path of virtue and peace. Experience is the rule by which we try everything. Many new things appear upon which we look with favor, but when experience lays them aside they are dead and beyond resurrection. All schools of philosophy on doubtful points are afraid of experience. From those points they try to frighten you like they would a child who cannot swim, by saying don't go there its deep water.

Reflection is a repetition of thought. If you pass a house, a grove of trees and an open field their image is imperfect in the memory. Pass them the second, the third and the fourth time and their image is perfected. Every board on the house, every leaning tree, the shades and shadows of the open field are treasured in the memory. This is reflection applied to the mental organ, the eye. When we are presented with a problem we pass it through the mind until all of its parts become familiar, and this is reflection upon any given problem by the mind.

Reason is comparison. Take two sticks, place them some distance apart and you are unable to determine which is the longest, because the distance between them disturbs in some degree the sense of vision. Place them together and you see at once which is the longest. This decides the sense of vision, and we decide all of our difficulties upon the same principle.

Our problems must all be brought together and measured. You may call it comparison, experience or reason.

To the frequent application of the terms reflection and reason we apply the term wisdom, which is the experience of the age, and of all the past ages of the world.

The Greeks and Romans personified wisdom by the Goddess Minerva, according to their faith. The Goddess Minerva ruled over the mental world, distributing to or withholding wisdom from mortal man.

Solomon, the celebrated King of the Jews, personified wisdom in his book of proverbs in the 8th chapter. He represents wisdom in council with the Creator.

And Aristotle, who lived three hundred years before the Christian era, asserted that human reason did not originate with the body, and that it was bestowed upon it from the outside.

You may trace the mind from the first indication, sensation and on to thought. Reflection, reason and wisdom, and whatever link you strike, 10 or 10,000, break the chain alike.

All of the different names that we have given to the manifestations of mind are produced by the same intellect, and that inte'lect is not produced by the digestion of food. It is an eternal principle pervading the universe. It is the dominion of mind over matter.

It is not my province or intention to dispute any man's religious faith. No man can work without faith. No man can live without faith. His family, his countrymen, the human race, are entitled to his love and esteem, but his faith is his own.

I would not raise a vandal hand against the invigorating name of liberty. It is every man's right to enjoy his own faith, because faith is the ferryman who sets us all across the dark river. The great interest of humanity—here—lies in conduct—and the great teacher said, men do not gather in grapes of thorns, or figs of thistles.

One more picture and the curtain falls.

Talk about the Free Thinkers, the Christians and the Infidels; through the long ages of the historic period, they have waged a war of words that you might haul by the cartload and fill a common barn—a pile of rubbish that would discourage and dismay the boldest student in the world. A man had as well undertake to circumnavigate the globe with a wheel-barrow as to read and understand all of the books that have been written and published on mental philosophy. It would be sacrilege to throw another grain of sand on this mountain of opinions, were it not a worthy heroism to teach man the value of his own mental freedom.

Our philosophy flows as freely as a river of water; we enter no man's brain for the purpose of taking a *prisoner;* we have no mysterious judgments—passed by a court of doubtful authority—to execute. Every man's brain is an Empire, duly commissioned and appointed to fight its own battles and work out its own destiny, whether he be a Baptist, Methodist or Presbyterian—whether his coat be taken from a Catholic or Protestant box, so it covers a true and faithful heart.

Our words are taken from Nature; our book is written by Nature's soft hand, and needs no interpreter. We speak the same language to every man, whether he be at the north pole or under the equator; whether his lot be cast upon a lone island in the sea, or among the crowded crowned heads of Europe; whether he be king, or subject, or a favored son of "the land of the free and home of the brave."

LECTURE IV.—MAN AND ANIMALS.

What little time we have, even in the longest life, for observation, and when we are confined to one spot on the earth, we only see the things that surround us and are peculiar to the place upon which we live. It is by the light of history that we see the actions of other men in other places and other ages of the world, and if we undertake to pass judgment upon the human race *without* the light of history, how *limited* our knowledge, how *unjust* our judgment. When we look back through the glass of history, though it may be dark in some places, and observe the actions of the distinguished men—among all nations and in all ages of the world, from the remotest historic period of antiquity to the present time—how much better prepared are we to pass judgment upon the character of man. History stamps virtuous and noble actions with the seal of applause; vicious and evil deeds with the indelible ink of infamy.

Brave and noble deeds, performed by heroes of a bygone age, stand as boldly forth as does a lighthouse on the shore of destiny; dark and unrelenting evils, performed by cowardly actors, is a warning to us and to all succeeding generations of men.

> While life and time shall pass away,
> The deeds of men are sure to stay;
> Impressions made on the sands of tim
> In every age and in every clime,
> Are covered not by time nor space
> But lasting as the human race.

Seven hundred and seventy-six years before the Christian era, Greek historians recorded the name of the victor in the Olympic games, and this is the first reliable date of ancient time. The Chaldean, the Egyptian, the Babylonian, the Assyrian and the Persian empires had their rise and fall, and left their remains for the future antiquarian to search in vain for the date of their rise or time of their glory.

The Jews crystalized on the western borders of Asia. Their laws forbade them to intermingle with other people, and they made no advance in civilization from the time Joshua led the Israelites over the river Jordan until Titus destroyed Jerusalem and Jewish nationality. The philosophy of the priests and rulers was carefully recorded and preserved in the archives of their temples. They paid little or no attention to time or dates.

A careful comparison of their records and traditions places the antiquity of man at about 7,320 years. Modern antiquarians think this time entirely too short—indeed, some have ventured to place the antiquity of man as far back as 24,000 years. How long man lived a purely animal life we have no means of knowing. Scientific men speak of three ages, which they denominate the "Stone," the "Bronze" and the "Iron" ages. In the infant age of the human race they made no tools of anything but stone—all of their implements were made of stone. At a more advanced period bronze appears, decorating their implements and ornaments.

With the "Iron Age" commences heroic civilization and the light of written history. This light first illuminated the hills of Greece. All Asia had been an immense battle-field. The Grecian States, on the edge of the great waves of conflict, emerged from the night of darkness. In this rude and barbarous age a knowledge of letters animated the men of Greece with the spirit of liberty. The Egyptian, Chinese and Hindoo people sought repose in non-intercourse, contented to remain in their own native darkness, reached a certain point of regulated order and stopped. The Chaldean, Assyrian and Persian races kept in the stream of progress.

The moving to and fro of great bodies of men, the wars of conquest and subjugation, gave rise to commerce. The intermingling of nations advanced civilization, while the desolating hand of war destroyed the identity of existing people. The intermingling of races gave rise to a nobler blood; and, with the letters of Greece and rise of Rome, we see the Caucasian race come upon the stage of action, unfolding the great work of genius and progress. How far they will ultimately go, lies way forward in the future womb of time.

Diverse from the course of the sun, human genius rises up in the West and flows toward the East. Alexander the Great rose up in the West and conquered the nations of the East; Constantine the Great rose up in the West and made himself master of the Roman Empire; Charlemagne restored the West long after the Eastern division of the Roman Empire perished. In all of the great battles of earth, the eagle of victory has hovered 'round western arms. In our late war, the flag of victory followed western men. The heart and soul of this country, is in the Mississippi Valley.

I demonstrated in my lecture on time and motion, that the human race approached the middle of the historic period, before any instrument was invented for keeping time. The ancients paid no attention to chronology. The Chaldean was the first empire. Abram, the father of the Jewish nation, went out from Ur, of the Chaldees, to go into the land of Canaan. He pre-empted the land of Canaan from the river Euphrates to the borders of Egypt. Subsequently we have the history of the patriarchs, preserved by tradition. Cities were built and walled in; temples and pyramids flourished and decayed, having stood as monuments of the power of kings, and slavery of the people.

After perusing the pages of book history, we turn to tradition—conflicting and contradicting accounts—turn us to cave history. We dig up the bones of our progenitors, marked only with long periods of time. The cradle of humanity is lost in the night of ages. The antiquarian is like a stranger in a strange land, who, after losing every trace of his way, wanders in the shades of night.

I come now to speak of the Romans, and of the Caucasian race. Alexander the Great, Julius Cæsar, Napoleon Bonaparte, and George Washington, were all descendants of the Caucasian race. Galileo, Sir Isaac Newton, Professor Morse and Benjamin Franklin, descended from the Caucasian race. All, or nearly all, of the men of progress, are descendants of the Caucasian race. There are a few among the Mongolians, less among the Malays, and none among the negro races of men. Rome was built on the bank of the river Tiber in Italy; there is nothing peculiar about its locality. It was the character of the people that made Rome the mistress of the world. You may trace that character from the Tiber, in Italy, to the Thames in England, and to the Potomac and Mississippi in America. Talk about a war of races. The barbarism of physical war is passing away. A war of intellect is coming upon the stage. This war will blend all nations in one language and one religion. Who shall the victor be? Let the Caucasian answer.

Julius Cæsar, although brave and generous, laid the foundation upon which was subsequently erected the great power of the Roman monarchs, the history of whom, furnish us with the outlines of vice and virture. Some of them have a high claim to virtue; none were ever false to their power, or unmindful of it. No man, either of high or low estate, could escape the frown of the Emperor. There was no country upon the habitable earth, to which he could fly, as the land of the free, and home of the brave. Go where he would, the frown of the Emperor followed him as dark as the valley of Hinnom and certain as the grasp of death—there was no escape from it, but in the Spirit Land, where humanity is laid even, and the servant is free from his master. The proud Roman, when defeated, never asked for or expected his life. To him defeat and death were the same thing. In the result of this philosophy, we see one hundred and fifty thousand Romans engaged in a single battle, not against a foreign enemy; it was Roman against Roman, steel against steel, Caucasian against Caucasian. The power of the Emperor was everything. Hence we see Brutus and Cassius in the Senate house with drawn daggers, not to spill the blood of Cæsar, but to waste the power of the Emperor. The history of the Roman Republic was fresh in the mind of Brutus, and he thought but one man (Julius Cæsar) stood in the way, and this has given rise to the classic words: "Not that I love Cæsar less; but I love Rome more." When, afterward, Brutus was overcome by the united arms of Antony and Octavius, he consecrated the declaration by throwing his body upon his sword, exclaiming: "O! virtue, thou art but a name!" History has embellished the name of Brutus as the noblest Roman of them all. With the fall of the Roman empire, we date the rise of modern nations. We have different countries, and different races of men—thousands of years have transpired in giving character to the different races. Our country stands pre-eminently in the front rank of all nations which are in the stream of progress. In most other countries men are born princes, they are born aristocrats and they are born workmen. In our country, a man is not born anything—he is born to fill the measure marked out by his capacity. We have done more, and we are doing more, than any other country, to develop the intellect of the individual man.

All the lessons of history teach us that man is a progressive being, and that in its infancy the human race, like the birth of the individual man, was born naked, with no institutions, destitute of all arts and sciences, and as some eminently learned men believe, speechless, from which condition he has ever been struggling up from the dark valley of antiquity to a high and holy hill of light. In childhood we believe the strange stories of our nurse; in manhood we discard the stories and retain our love for the nurse. We love the old men who nursed the infancy of humanity, but we are discarding their strange stories. The early traditions of all nations, surround the accounts of their origin with supernatural persons and events, which the judgment of more enlightened times, condemn as fabulous and impossible. The primitive condition of the human race is represented by very opposite opinions. One claims a golden age of innocence and bliss, the other a wild and savage state of barbarism. There must have been a first man, and it matters but little to us, whether we adopt the dirt philosophy, that he was made of clay, or the evolution theory, that he developed from the lower animals, When he became man, he was not an animal nor an angel. Standing on a middle ground between the animal and angelic state, no wonder he ate forbidden fruit. No wonder his appetite continues for so many generations. The greater wonder is, that he is emerging from the slavery of his appetite, and traveling on toward the temple of knowledge. Standing way back in the twilight of the infancy of the race, he may have resembled a speechless brute of the forest, making his desires known to those at hand in a barbarous dialect, and eking out a life-time in the neighborhood of his native cave. Now he speaks to his fellow-man across the ocean, traverses a continent in a few days, and circumnavigates the globe in a few months. All history teaches that man is progressive, and points out the difficulties that have been overcome—those that yet stand in the way—and that these achievements are being accomplished by universal education.

We come now to speak more definitively of *man and animals*, as seen on the broad field of nature with the *naked eye*. Let us take man down to a level with the animals. Not that we wish to degrade humanity, but for the sake of the argument let us take man down to a level with the animals. They see by the same light, hear by the same means, feel by the same process, feed upon the same food, drink the same water, breathe the same air, and are animated by the same mental elements. Where, then, is the great mental difference between men and between animals and man? Is it not in their physical and mental organism?

Take a transparent bottle, fill it with beautiful trinkets, and you see all of their variegated colors. Then take an opaque or blue bottle, fill it with the same trinkets, and you will hardly distinguish one trinket from another—yet all that you see in the blue bottle, you see by the same light that you see them in the transparent bottle. Then, is not the difference in the organism of the two bottles containing the trinkets? And I affirm that the mental difference between men and between animals and man, is in the casket containing the mental trinkets—the size, nature and quality of the *brain*. The man who undertakes to overthrow this philosophy will have a blue-bottle head; for he will begin by telling you about a spirit, or some dark, incomprehensible thing. The dog is more intelligent than the cat. Is there a dog spirit and a cat spirit? or is the difference in the mental organism of the two animals? A dog acts upon the basis of his mental organism, and so does a man. A dog barks and hunts, like his ancestors did 2,000 years ago, because he has no mental organ of progress. Animal instinct is the great hobby-horse of old philosophers. What is instinct? A rose will smell as sweet by any other name. They say instinct, and there they stop. What they call instinct is nothing but a *mental organ* transmitted from one generation to another. We find it in all animals, and also in man, wise by inheritance. The bee builds a honey cell to-day, like its ancestors did 2000 years ago. This knowledge in the bee is a mental organ, transmitted by inheritance. Go with me to a beaver's dam, and you will observe the beaver has not only selected a good locality on the creek—he has also taken every advantage of the ground—he has executed his work like his ancestors did ages ago. And the old philosophers call it instinct. They have drawn a line between what they have been pleased to call *instinct* and *reason*.

It is like the axle we put through the earth, upon which we say the earth revolves—it has no existence, in reality. A man who is born blind, is mentally inferior to one born with eyes—that is, he has one brain organ less. And we must draw the line between man and animals upon the basis of mental organism. But you must remember that neither man nor animal can learn or realize anything that does not come within the scope of some of his mental organs. Show a beautiful picture to a blind man, or whisper the soft voice of love in the ear of a deaf woman, and what do you accomplish? Men learn to the extent of their mental organism, and so do animals; and both receive knowledge by inheritance.

In all ages of the world there have been men, wise by inheritance. They manifest their wisdom by a fixed organ in the brain. Their ideas of the way things ought to be performed, their philosophy of time and space of men and things of humanity, and human destiny, with them is all settled—was known to their fathers and transmitted to them by inheritance. These men never give anything to art, science, or philosophy. They are like the bee and the beaver—willing to work like their ancestors did ages ago.

Man has a mental organ of progress, of which we will

speak in our next lecture more at length. It is a law of nature, that like produces like, and by the force of this law all of our mental organs receive an impulse in the blossom. Primitive man commenced by cutting things with a sharp stone. As genius and discoveries advanced, tools were improved, and necessity demanded workmen in wood, stone and metal. Continual work, and consequently continued thought on the best way to work, strengthened the mental organ of mechanism; and that organ in an active state—has been transmitted from one generation to another, until now we have children born mechanics. We may say the same of music—we have children born musicians, and we have children born honest, and born rogues, and where will we stop? This we call the laws of hereditary descent—they defy and resist education for a long time. Take a child that is a born rogue—one in whom the organ or passion to steal has been strongly fixed by inheritance, and it meets with no strenuous opposition as the boy grows up—he will steal whether he be needy or not. Confine him in prison for theft, and when you let him out he will steal again. You might put him in a wake, to sit up with the dead, and he would steal the ornaments from his grandmother's coffin.

An honest man cannot steal—he don't know how—because he has not received the passion by inheritance or instruction.

All of our knowledge is directed by mental organism; for knowledge is the same thing throughout the broad expanse of the mental world—an animal knows what it does know as well as a man. The brain of an animal is less extensive than the brain of a man, and does not realize as many facts. Attack a man and his dog. The dog will realize the fact that you are an enemy, as quick as the man, though he may not know all of the facts in the case. The humblest individual in this house knows that the door opens on the east side of the building just as well as the wisest philosopher in this assembly knows that fact. His opportunities may have been limited, but so far as his understanding has realized facts, he knows the truth of those facts just as well as the most accomplished and learned man in the world.

Our difference in knowledge is in *quantity*, and not in *quality*. Some men have a more extensive mental organism than others, arising from inheritance, instruction and opportunity, and may acquire more knowledge—that is more in quantity, but of no better quality.

The mental organism of some races of men is more extensive than other races. The teachers of the negro race in this country will bear testimony that that race cannot be educated, up to the Caucasian standard of education. Their limited mental organism cannot penetrate the wonderful avenues that have been traced by Caucasian brain.

Seeing, hearing, tasting, smelling and feeling, are the five senses of the old philosophers. They are common to animals and man. They are all external and visible organs of the brain. Sensation or feeling, in some of our mental organs, is the object and aim of all humanity. Too many delight in the sensation of appetite, they explore the kitchen from the pantry to the slop-bucket to find something that will stimulate the appetite. Others more intent after something to stimulate other feelings, can live a week on a sea-biscuit and a woodpecker.

The internal as well as the external organs of the brain, are seen in animals, as in man, but are more extensive in man. The passions always manifest themselves with the character of the mental organ through which they pass. Anger frowns and stamps, grief wrings its hands, joy dances and leaps. Self-esteem throws the body in an erect, proud attitude; combativeness throws the body of a man or animal in the attitude of attack. The dog opens his mouth and shows his teeth, man doubles up and shows his fist to his adversary. The sensation of fear or cowardice throws the body in a stooping, watchful position. The dog sneaks off with his tail down, and to use a slang phrase, man *skedadles*.

All of our feelings assume the character of the brain organ, through which they pass, and manifest themselves according to the strength of that organ. Our mental organs become feeble when left out of use, and strong when cultivated. Boys who grow up in the streets, without the watchful care of a faithful mother, learn the lessons of idleness, and receive impressions on the infant brain, eminently calculated to produce in age, a regular *soup-house-rat*.

Boys who grow up at home and in the schools, get the foundation of a better education; kind parents and a pleasant home, sow the seed of patriotism and love of country. When the precious jewels of the infant brain are unfolded by the delicate touch of a faithful mother, the noble woman has not only served her child, she has served her country, God, and the human race.

When you hear a man say he is not in favor of the common schools, that he is a bachelor, and don't take the county paper, you may set him down in the dead-book; too penurious to educate the orphan; too mean to have a son of his own; too careless to read the events transpiring 'round him; will give nothing for the fate of his country, or life of his nation; unwilling to contribute one drop of oil to the light of the age in which he lives—he is a *dead beat*.

The wheel of progress moves too slow, yet it rolls steadily on. The work is assigned to a few individuals, who are in the main public men, giving precept and example. In all ages and countries they make mistakes. No stream was ever known to rise above its fountain. When the ruling or leading men of society, or of a nation, indulge in vice, the public mind is poisoned at the fountain and all the streams become impure. The human brain is stamped with the love of imitation. Our wise men look back for a precedent. We measure our actions by the laws of the society in which we live. Individual effort to rise above the laws of society is dimly discernable. No wonder virtuous humanity has struggled so long and so hard.

Some scientific men have endeavored to identify man and animals, by appealing to the body. They have dissected the brain, counted the teeth and measured the bones of all the monkeys, under the false impression that brain produces mind. The Darwinian theory of improvement by natural selection as applied to the animal kingdom, is founded upon laborious study and profound philosophy, but it applies to the body and not to the mind. We have improved our domestic animals to a wonderful extent, but that improvement applies to the body and not to the mind. If you want a wise hog you must go back to the old wood-rooter. Cultivating the body does not always cultivate the mind. If it did, the man who could make the grandest bodily show, would be the wisest man in the world.

In the third century of the Christian era there lived a Roman Emperor—Maximin—of Gothic origin, who was said to be eight feet high, could drink seven gallons of wine and eat forty pounds of meat in a day. He could grind up pebbles in the palm of his hands and tear up a small tree by the roots. Yet his mind was not sufficiently developed to command the Roman legions, for he was murdered in his tent by some of his own soldiers. The Greeks and Romans educated their youth in physical strength, that they might become good soldiers. Mental education was little thought of among the ancients, especially the education of the masses. We have fine institutions of learning, but we have too many book-men, and too few original men.

Too many travel in the beaten path of their predecessors

and never stop to think of original things. You must think. The tide of thought flows as freely as the atmosphere, but you don't use it. You had as well try to realize physical strength without action, as to try to realize mental strength without thinking. But remember you had as well try to trace a bee course in the backwoods without eyes, or fly from the Black Hills to the Dead Sea without wings, as try to learn or realize anything, for which you have no mental capacity. Go on with the natural bent of the mind. Press forward in the direction that the light appears, and on, and on, you will go, for the poet said:

"Man's greatest knowledge is himself to know."

All men soon become acquainted with their bodies But as I have already demonstrated, the body is not the man, the mind is the man

I once knew an old man by the name of Vincen who was in the habit of getting drunk, as we say, and as you all know, this operation is performed by driving the mind out of the brain and leaving the body to take care of itself, without the mind to direct it. The poor body is found wanting. Can't walk straight. Don't know up from down. It is all the time going down, and all the time going up; but goes down, more than it does up. We call it drunk. It is the body that is drunk, not the mind. The mind has left the body limber and we call it drunk.

Old man Vincen lived in the country, and he went to town where he met with his brother, who gave him a new coat. After this event he met some drinking friends and got drunk. In this condition his body started home in the dusk of the evening. On the way, when the last lingering spark of mind had departed, the question presented itself to that body: Had Vincen started home, or was he yet in town? The eyes surveyed the body: the new coat looked strange, the lips muttered, this is not Vincen, Vincen is in town. Who can this be? God! this is Shaw. Shaw was a proud, dressy man. The legs of that body raised the feet high to walk like Shaw, and it tumbled into a mud hole, where it lay until the next morning, when old man Vincen came and dragged it out.

Oh! how many drive the mind away from them by intoxication. Oh! how many, by mental laziness, fail to prepare the mental house, prepare the store-houses of the brain, and the mind or the man will come and dwell in it. And let me say to all young men, do not sit down and brood over the opinion that you are no great man, for if such be the case, you have made no preparation for a great mind to come and dwell in your brain. Go to work, clear away the rubbish, forsake all of your bad habits. We do not see great men seek the company of rowdies, then drive the rowdies, the bad habits out of your brain, and a great mind will come and dwell there.

When the mental element enters, brain organism, it produces sensation or feeling. All live animals have feeling, but of very different character. The horse has a sensation of hunger, but he has no sensation of honor or honesty; he will eat another horse's corn as quick as his own.

Then I ask, what mysterious power produces all of the various sensations, passions and feelings, that we observe in the animal kingdom, where can you place it but with brain organism?

An animal, through his brain organs, realizes the sensations of hunger, thirst, rest, association, love, hatred, ambition and fear, in common with man.

Man, through a superior brain organism, realizes the additional sensations of honor, honesty, happiness, holiness, integrity, industry and immortality.

The old philosophy of instinct and reason that man

learns, and that animals do not, is a mistake that must be apparent to all men of experience with animals, who think at all. An animal can be taught to the extent of its mental organism. In teaching an animal we always appeal to sensation or feeling. We must appeal to a mental organ of which he is in possession, sight, smell, hearing, love, fear, appetite or any other mental organ common to his species, in some of which he is superior to man. Your dog can tell you the course the rabbit runs, when you can not tell by the use of the same means; because nature has given him a more refined sensation in one of his mental organs—the nose. Man has circumnavigated the globe, measured the earth and fathomed the sea; has raised his arm to the clouds and brought down the lightning to his use; can speak to his fellow man across the ocean and detail the momentous events of the day. And yet he is compelled to sit down in the glory of all his wisdom, and acknowledge that his dog knows some things that he does not know.

The most accomplished statesman that ever erected a legal standard on the face of God's green earth, or presided over the highest and best appointed institution of learning ever organinized among mankind may learn some things from a poor, forlorn, ragged and wretched beggar. Teaching is unfolding the great casket of nature. No mortal man has ever seen the last picture. We clean the dust out of our eyes with a towel and water; teaching is cleaning the dust out of our mental organs with the water of experience; but you had as well try to unfold the brilliancy of the sun to a blind man, as try to teach a man or an animal anything that is outside of his mental organs. You had as well try to frighten the man in the moon from crossing the ocean without a canoe, as try to teach a man or an animal anything for which he has no mental capacity. You may soon teach a dog to sit by the fire, because his feelings soon realize the advantage of heat, but you cannot teach him to mend up the fire, because his limited mental organism does not permit him to see cause while it does not realize effect. Man soon learns to build up the fire, but if you ask him what fire is—he like the dog—he can't tell you.

Pliny, Mola and Plutarch speak of ancient tribes in Egypt, Greece and Persia, who were unacquainted with the use of fire. Chinese historians acknowledge the same of their progenitors, the inhabitants of the Marian islands discovered in 1551, who made no use of fire, and the friction match was not discovered until 1829, by John Walker. The old people used to keep the seed of fire, as they called it, covered up in the ashes, and when the seed was lost, hunt up a flint and strike like Pittsburg, not for more wages, but more fire. Now you can buy a box of matches with a cent, and set the city on fire, like the strikers at Pittsburg; turn the iron horse; but if we ask you what fire is, you are like the dog, you can't tell. Fire is an old friend as well as an enemy. We have known it always, but we only know its name. We know that is a principle or element pervading the universe. More than this we do not know, because our limited mental organism does not permit us to penetrate the secret chambers of the universe of God.

One more lecture and we part. Friends are parting throughout our beautiful land. Friends live forever, and love forever, but they do not part forever. They part like a city and the sun, to meet again in a little while. You and I part at death, and what is our life? One line in the great book of history; one grain in the sands of time; one drop in the ocean of humanity, and adieu to the scene we call life. We part in trouble; we meet in peace; we part in a world of sin and sorrow; we meet in a world of purity and peace; we part in tenements of clay; we meet in tenements immortalized. This closes our lecture on man and animals. Our next ecture is on spirit and soul, in which we will speak of the mental organ we term the organ of progress.

> More intricate than the broad expanse of the universe,
> The hidden friend and wonderful counselor of all nations of men
> That has ever been as true to the barbarous as to civilized man;
> That has stood over the dusky woman of ancient times,

and hovers 'round the accomplished mother of our civilization, when she lays the darling of her bosom beneath the dark, green sod, and will ever stand over the last lingering spark of humanity, until the sun of hope darkens and disappears from the heaven of anticipations.

LECTURE V.—SPIRIT AND SOUL.

Brutus will start a spirit as soon as Cæsar.— Shakspeare.

In our previous lectures we endeavored to look at nature in a natural way. The present subject seems to demand that we should depart, at least in some degree, from the great cardinal principles laid down by the laws of nature, yet we do not propose to travel on the out-side track. True to our nature and to the laws that govern the universe, we will travel upon that road as long as there is a foot of ground beneath our feet, and when the last grain of sand has sunk from our pathway, make one long leap for the eternal shore.

In the language of St. Paul—"If we have hope only in this life, we are of all men most miserable."

The errors of our fathers are left behind in the backwoods. We have thrown the old stage coach away, and pass from city to city on a palace car; but we have not thrown away the principle. We have improved the roads, magnified the motive power, and enlarged the coach, but we still travel upon wheels.

Many great minds of the age have thrown away the philosophy of primitive Judaism, but there is a principle in human nature that they cannot throw away without throwing themselves away, for it was planted by that great eternal hand who laid the foundations of the universe, and appointed a place for the earth.

In the early dawn of the historic period Jacob journeyed toward Haran, and slept under a tree, with the grass for a bed and a stone for a pillow. He dreamed that he saw a ladder reaching from Earth to Heaven. This is the second dream recorded in Jewish history. No one will contend that Jacob saw a material ladder. That ladder was seen by the mind's eye, or by the great power of the imagination; and, although it was not a true ladder, it did represent a true principle.

The imagination is a principle in mental organism common to all men. It is no true philosophy to claim it for any profession or class of men to the exclusion of all others. It is the foundation upon which all of the castles of superstition known to the human race have been erected. No man builds a house without a foundation, and any philosophy not founded upon some of the cardinal principles of nature, is nothing but a castle in the air.

If any man will show me how the human understanding can be approached, out-side of the natural senses common to all men, by any other avenue than that of imagination, I will never open my mouth again on the subject of mental philosophy. When a man has long dissipated he sometimes sees snakes in his boots. Now we all know that the snakes are false, but the principle is not false. The sight of the snakes is a picture, representing the road of ruin and dissipation upon which the mind is traveling. The power of the mind called imagination underlies all human progress. It represents genius and forecast as well as spirit and soul. A steam engine would have run as well two thousand years ago as it does to-day, and the magnetic telegraph would have conveyed language across the ocean on the day that Columbus discovered America, just as well and upon the same principles that it does to-day. But those principles in nature slumbered beneath a dark cloud of ignorance for ages.

The question naturally presents itself to us: by what means do we penetrate the dark recesses of the universe and unfold the secret nerves of nature so useful to man? Let the man of genius answer, and he will tell you before he made any new thing, he saw its picture with the mind's eye, or by the great power of imagination. And thus through the long ages of the historic period that great power of the mind, the imagination, has been unfolding the beauties of nature, and no man can say that we have approached the end of the chapter, or even the middle of the casket.

Could the wisest philosopher of the age sleep a thousand years and reappear upon the stage of action, he would be lost in wonder, and look upon the age in which we live as an age of semi-barbarism.

On the sixth day of October, 1829, George Stephenson, a coal miner of Northumberland, England, having constructed the *Rocket*, the first locomotive engine ever seen in the world, run it from Manchester to Liverpool at the rate of thirty miles an hour. All practical mechanics in the country, while Stephenson was at work, condemned the experiment and pronounced it a failure. George Stephenson saw the picture of the *Rocket* by the power of his imagination before he made the engine, for no man can work in the dark. At this period the great Henry Clay was wasting his eloqence in Congress, in favor of the Cumberland turnpike road. Mr. Clay was a great orator, but he was no mechanic. Hence we see the dusty coal miner coming forward with an argument more potent than all the oratory in the world.

I do not contend that every picture presented to the imagination can be worked out. There must necessarily be failures among all men and among all classes.

All Bible readers are familar with the book of Daniel. Daniel saw four beasts rise up out of the sea, and the fourth beast was diverse from the rest. He had great iron teeth and ten horns, and soon there came up among them another little horn that had eyes. No one will contend that Daniel saw any beast in reality; he saw a picture by the great power of imagination, which he said was a picture of a revolution in governments. Daniel was a prisoner in Babylon, and his mind glowed with unabating tenacity for a return to his native land. Learned clergymen have been trying to work out Daniel's pictures for more than two thousand years. The angel Gabriel, so often mentioned by subsequent writers, whom they have commissioned to sound the last horn, is one of Daniel's pictures. Daniel is the first writer who mentions the name of the angel Gabriel, which you may see by consulting the book of Daniel, viii. 15. It is said that Daniel's book was shown to Alexander the Great, and he supposed that he saw his own image in one of Daniel's pictures, and for this cause treated the Jews with great lenity.

The old Jews taught their descendants that some animals were unclean, and their laws forbade the use of them. All historians know with what great respect the Jews regarded their laws. We read in the Christian Scriptures that Peter, when he dwelt at Joppa, with Simon, a tanner, by the sea side, saw a great sheet, held at four corners, and let down from heaven; this sheet was full of all manner of beasts, and he heard a voice saying, "Arise, Peter, kill and eat." No one believes that Peter saw a real sheet full of real animals. Peter saw a picture, by the great power of imagination, from which he concluded that the God of the Jews was also the God of the Romans, for he soon after baptized Cornelius, who was a Roman. We know that the question prevailed at that time among some of the early Christians, whether or not their faith extended outside of the Jewish nation.

St. John said: "I stood upon the sand of the sea and saw a beast rise up out of the sea having seven heads and ten horns." No one believes that any such beast ever had an existence in the universe. St. John saw a picture by the great power of his imagination. Many have wondered at the similarity between the visions of Daniel and St. John. Daniel lived 700 years before St. John, and Alexander the Great, who lived 300 years before St. John, supposed that he saw himself in one of Daniel's pictures. Some of the clergymen of our day are engaged in working out those pictures. They are like the boy who went out to learn French when he did not understand his mother tongue.

Mind operates upon or through brain organism, and all of these old men, who have long since passed away and gone to their reward, were mentally organized precisely like men are to-day. When thought has long impressed any of the mental organs the imagination extends in the direction of that organ.

Mahomet went into a cave and secluded himself, while his imagination traversed the regions of heaven, astraddle of a white mule. A mechanic may train his thoughts upon the subject of invention until they travel, seemingly, out side of his brain, and he beholds wonderful associations of machinery—he is in the broad field of imagination where every shape and form appears. This great power of the human brain is common to all men. One class of men reveal the beauties of heaven, another class reveal the beauties of earth. We call them the *men of progress.*

A word is the sign or garment of an idea. Living languages are progressive. No language has ever lived a thousand years. Could the subjects of Alfred the Great reappear in England they would not understand the English language as it is spoken to-day. Much difficulty sometimes arises from the want of a proper understanding of the words we speak. I hold my hand here, and move it there. My hand is a thing and will perish, the change of its position is a principle and will not perish; thus you will understand what

I mean by the words *things* of nature and *principles* of nature.

I come now to speak of the word *spirit*, and will endeavor and do so in a spirit of meekness.

The word spirit occurs in the Scriptures about 324 times, and is generally used to designate a principle, and not a thing. The word angel is often used in the Scriptures, and designates a body or thing. The word soul occurs in the Scriptures about 220 times. It is often used to designate a number or individual—eight souls, or eight persons, crossed over the flood in Noah's ark. We conclude, therefore, that the word spirit, as we should understand it, designates a principle or a picture, and not a body or thing. When a whole nation are of one opinion with regard to anything, we call that principle the spirit of the age, or of the nation. We say, the common schools are upheld by the spirit of the age.

I know that a great many persons individualize spirits, and think they have seen them. It is said Martin Luther once threw his ink-stand at the *devil*, and the ink-stand went through the devil, and hit the wall of his room. He threw his ink-stand at a picture; that picture was false, but it did represent a principle. The old man was worried with his enemies and saw their picture, to which his imagination gave the shape of the devil.

There are many persons who believe in what they call "the operation of the Spirit." This philosophy in one sense is true. When a number of individuals all meet together, having concentrated their thoughts upon devotion by a law of nature, impressions long continued upon a mental organ will carry the mind in that direction, and sometimes it will pass out into the broad field of imagination. The operation of the Spirit must be upon or through mental organism. If the impressions are made upon the good organs of the brain the spirit will be good. And if the impressions are made upon the bad organs of the brain the manifestations will be that of a bad spirit.

The Pharisees, a religious sect among the Jews, who flourished immediately before the Christian era, taught the philosophy of the existence of a spirit, or soul, in man, disconnected and separate from the body or mind, and of course must be deaf and dumb, *incognito* and foolish, *this is the darkest picture of all of the dark ages.* The word spirit should always be applied to the mind, and never to, the body. Wherever we find mind we find spirit. We never say the spirit of a tree, but we do say, a dull and high-spirited horse, and a dull and high-spirited man. When one is dead we say his spirit is gone, or has left the body. It is a clumsy philosophy to apply a material body to the existence of spirit. What can the Christian say who believes in the resurrection of the body? Will he not, when the spirit body and the human body meet, cry out: "O, wretched spirit that I am, who shall deliver me from these material bodies?" When the mind is gone the spirit goes with it, and when the mind returns the spirit returns with it. A spirit separated from the mind is the ghost of superstition; was born in a dark corner of the field of fear, with reversed eyes—can see in the night, but sleeps in the day; fed on credulity, lived through the dark ages, and may yet be seen in dark places through the dark glasses of modern spiritualism. When the last dark corner of the human brain becomes illuminated it will bid adieu to the earth forever.

The meek and lowly Jesus, the great moral Teacher whose standard of morality is truly the best the world ever saw, He who spake as never man spake, used the word spirit only *eleven times.* Those who wrote his history used it a great many more times. Jesus used it eleven times, that is recorded in the Scriptures. He used it always in the same, or nearly the same sense. The first time he used it was in the sermon on the mount. He said, "Blessed are the poor in spirit, for theirs is the kingdom of heaven." The last time he used it was on the cross, when the last mortal wound had been inflicted. He said, "*Father, into thy hands I commend my spirit.*"

No. I am mistaken. He used it once after this. You will find it in the last chapter of Luke, commencing at the 36th verse.

His scholars, the apostles, were all together in a certain place, soon after the crucifixion, holding a council on the perils of the times. The Master had been executed, no one could tell the fate of his followers; they were all afraid of the multitude and of public authority. The spirit of persecution was abroad in the land. The germ of Christianity was in that little council, and of this meeting the text reads: "And as they spake Jesus himself stood in the midst of them and saith 'unto them, '*Peace be unto you,*' but they were terrified and affrighted, and supposed they had seen a spirit, and he said unto them, 'Why are ye troubled and why do thoughts arise in your hearts? Behold my hands and my feet, that it is I myself, handle me and see, for a spirit hath not flesh and bones, as you see me have,' and for further proof he did eat before them."

The idea of a material spirit originated with the Pharisees. The early Christian writers founded their philosophy on the resurrection of the human body, and this is not in conflict with the true philosophy of spirit. There is nothing in the wide world, so dear to a Christian, as a Christian's hope. The man who would wantonly disfigure a Christian's hope, would steal the family casket of his grandmother, and disfigure the fair faces of those who gave him being. The sum of that hope is in the resurrection of the human body; the infant form, the darling body, that has been laid beneath the green carpet to sleep, shall be restored again, to the bosom of its mother, in the resurrection of the dead.

St. Paul said, when speaking of the Christian's hope, in the eighth chapter of Romans: "We groan within ourselves, waiting for the adoption, to wit: the resurrection of our body.' Josephus, the learned historian of the Jews, in expounding the laws of *Moses*, uses this language: "God hath made this grant, to those who observe these laws, even though they be obliged to die for them, that they shall come into being again, and at a certain revolution of things receive a better life, than they had enjoyed before.

Infidelity, the love of the marvelous, and the hope of gain, are the nest eggs of modern disembodied spirits. The broad and open field of imagination is where the nest was found. Andrew Jackson Davis sat on the eggs. This great apostle of clairvoyance, Som-nam-bu-lism, som-nil-o-quence, and all other sleeping beauties of the brain, says on the twenty-first page of his work, entitled, *The Principles of Nature*: "Seven times I have been requested to explain the nature and composition of spirit." Then after making some remarks on the different characters of men, he continues; "Follow me through this investigation, and then decide according to the evidence you receive, for, or against the conclusions arrived at." This modest request of Mr. Davis was to follow him through 782 pages. I followed him, and can best give you my experience by relating an anecdote.

"During the early settlement of Kentucky, in the infant age of the dark and bloody ground, when our great-grandfathers and great-grandmothers were rocked in a sugar trough and the children played around the log-cabin, which was adorned with turkey-wings and buck horns, an early settler cleared off five acres of ground, around which he made a new rail fence, so close that a rabbit could not crawl through it. He planted it in corn, and in the early fall while walking 'round his field, discovered that hogs had been destroying the crop. He examined every panel of the fence, to find where the brute had entered the field. There was a ravine or natural ditch through the field, and when building the fence across this ravine, a hollow linn log was thrown in, to partly fill up the ditch, and the fence was placed upon it. Our farmer had a neighbor, who owned a spotted shoat, and if there is a wise hog in the world, you will always find him in the shape of a *spotted shoat*. This fellow had crawled through the linn log and torn down four times as much corn as twenty hogs could eat, and contrary to hog nature, had crawled out through the same hole that he crawled in. When our farmer discovered the trick, he pulled the fence down off the log and endeavored to remove it, it was a crooked log—like my elbow—and the man succeeded in getting both ends of the log on the outside of the field and replaced the fence upon it. He then left the field, directing his attention to the spotted shoat. When the animal supposed the coast was clear, he cautiously approached the right end of the log and crawled through, coming out on the same side of the fence, when he raised his bristles and trotted off. He never went back to that field.

With the diligence of a hopeful student I waded through 782 pages of Mr. Davis' work, and like the spotted shoat, came out on the same side of the fence.

I spoke in my lecture on Time and Motion, of a great castle, in which allusion was made to the future state of man. This picture has existed among all nations of men.

"The soul uneasy and confined from home—
Rests, and expatiates in a life to come."

Mr. Davis proclaimed, that this castle was accessible, and beckoned his hearers to follow him. I followed him seven-hundred and eighty-two miles through the brush, it is true there was an occasional wild flower along the path-way. The journey was tedious and wearisome, at last the wall of the castle appeared in the distance, I struggled up to the door, Mr. Davis opened it, and I passed through, only to find myself in the woods on the other side. And Davis at last is compelled to come to the cold naked truth, and acknowledge that the interior of the castle is invisible until you go to sleep. He ought to be called, the sleeping beauty of the nineteenth century.

The definition of the word *medium*, is to stand in or about the middle. If an orator offering to address you, standing at so great a distance you could not hear him, and I stood in the middle—between you—repeating what he said, I would be a medium. Thus the spiritual medium, standing on the brink of the dark river, scanning the distant shores, sees, or thinks he sees, the golden edge of the new-born day, and with a cheek that knows no shame, reveals to credulous ears the mysteries of the spirit land. There have been mediums in all ages of the world. The late revival of spiritual mediums in this country, is eminently calculated to start civilization on the *back track*.

What is a medium? Let us dissect him. He is nothing but a bundle of poor humanity, feeds on the same food, breathes the same air and is animated by the same elements that animate all men. Has he not arms, and legs, a face, and a brain? In what is he different from other men? In nothing, but wearing a cheek that knows no shame.

Let us teach man the power of his own mental faculties, let him hear the voice of freedom it will elevate him above the power of principalities—and devils. The beauties of nature, the flowers of reason, the roses of happiness lie in reckless profusion along his path-way, he must gather them with his own hands. "Let me pluck them for you," is the voice of slavery. When you meet sin and sorrow make no appeal to community, community is as destitute of mercy, as the waves of the sea to a sinking ship. If you would ride boldly over the waves of trouble, you must paddle your own canoe. Every man thinks, or should think for himself. The tide of thought flows as freely as a river of water, it is the water of life, springing up to every man's brain. Oh! how bitter it is sometimes made from another's cup.

The life of the body is a forced state, a state of worry, of care and oft of sorrow and of weeping.

The life of the spirit comes a volunteer. We have already demonstrated life to be a development that belongs to the vegetable as well as the animal kingdom. The life of the spirit is a mental power eternal in itself pervading the universe.

The principles of nature are eternal. The power of the steam engine is a principle—the steam is a thing, the power a principle.

Honor arises from action, yet honor is a principle. One may have the external appearance of a gentleman, but if we find that he lacks the principle of honor we discard him. The things of nature perish or change form, the principles of failure are eternal.

The rocks we dig out of the mountain bear indisputable evidence that they once existed in another form.

The animals exist in the vegetable kingdom, and are developed into bodies of flesh and blood, and perish or change form. "Dust thou art, and unto dust thou shalt return," alludes alone to the body. The spirit never was and never can be dust.

Smoke rises up because it is lighter than the air; it acted the same way when the first fire was kindled upon the earth.

I speak to you to-day. My body will perish and return to dust after it has moldered beneath the sod for 2,000 ages. The same ideas may be advanced by another man, without any knowledge of me or of my record. The bodies of men and their language perish; but ideas do not perish, because mind is an eternal principle pervading the universe. Spirit is the flower of the mind. Who would have a foolish spirit? We come now to speak of the presence of the spirit in the mind for no philosopher can find spirit in anything else. You see with both eyes alike because you use both alike. Put a bandage over one for a week and you will not be able to see with it at all for a time. What is true of the eye is also true of the other mental organs. Put a bandage over your evil organs and the devil will not enter. Close the door against him and he will go away.

But, says one, I would do good but evil is present with me. It is hard to rid the mind of that old serpent—the Tempter.

This reminds me of the Arkansas doubter. There lived a man in the State of Arkansas whom all his neighbors called the doubter. He doubted everything, doubted the existence of the man in the moon. Some said that he doubted public opinion.

A traveler met the doubter in the road, and addressing him said:

"Sir, can you tell me where John Smith lives?"

The doubter, looked serious, replied "Do you see this bayou?"

"Yes."

"Well, this bayou runs west about three miles and then turns and runs south; right at the turn of the bayou there is a bridge; cross that bridge and you strike a high plain sloping gradually to the west; the road runs across that plain in a west direction; there are houses on each side of the road; John Smith may live in one of these houses, but I doubt it"

"I was not asking for your doubts, I want information."

"Well cross this plain in a west direction and you come to a large canebrake; pass through this canebrake and you strike a group of low flat hills, thickly settled; John Smith may live there, but I doubt it. They say that John Smith lives in all neighborhoods; strike any settlement, and by diligent inquiry you can find John Smith, but I doubt it."

"Go to the devil with your doubts," said the man, and started on.

"Hold on, stranger, I can tell you where John Smith does live. He lives in his own house, and if you can find that house, you will find where John Smith lives."

I am like the Arkansas doubter. You may go to church in search of a good spirit and you may find it there, but I doubt it. You may unfold the pages of ancient history in search of a good spirit, and you may find it there, but I doubt it. Hold, reader, I can tell you where you can find it—in its own house. Clear the rubbish out of your own brain; quit all of your bad conduct; prepare the residence for a good spirit, and it will come and dwell with you.

But, says one, morality is dead without religion. With profound regard for the religious schools of the day, I criticise this declaration. Morality comes strictly within the pale of mental philosophy, because it is the result of mental organism. The ancient definition of the word religion was to bind together. Our country and all other countries are full of churches and clergymen. They all teach religion. They all bind their own people together and leave humanity as wide apart as the poles. Morality is as broad as the earth, and beautiful as the unfolded heavens. The majestic idea of the word can march through the church and the state house; can enter the dark prison and comfort the lowly and down-trodden; can travel without a passport among all nations, and through all countries; can be spoken in every language and treasured in every heart. I would like to see all men everywhere religious; but religion without morality is like a bird sitting on marbles—marbles never hatch. Associations of men who have bound themselves together and claim exclusive jurisdiction over the great spirit should not crucify morality It comes like the mild teacher who appeared in Palestine to strengthen the weak and bind up the broken-hearted.

When I hear a man say that morality is dead without religion I think of that mild passage in the history of Jesus when his apostles came to him and said, "Master, we saw one casting out devils in thy name who did not follow us and we forbade him."

I think of the old Jews who supposed themselves in possession of all the genuine religion that was in the world, when justice would have released Jesus. They cried aloud to Pontius Pilate, "crucify him! crucify him! let his blood be upon us and upon our children." Individuality crucified morality.

Individuality is the rock upon which all theologians split. It has scattered the Christian church into more than 600 denominations, and throughout the globe the future state has been fitted to the human passions. Who can individualize the mind? a bundle of passions, desires, hopes and fears. Who can individualize spirit? We hope to meet our friends in the spirit land, but we do not hope to meet all of their individual passions. When we see outside of individuality we will be no longer individuals.

While man lives upon the earth he has a local habitation and a name. When he crosses the dark river he is borne away on the wide wings of hope through the stars and space. *Deo favente ad infinitum.*

Individuality is human and peculiar to humanity, in proof of which I appeal to the history of the old Jewish prophets. All will agree that they were animated by the same spirit, yet we find as much difference between them as we find in any other class of men. Some of them dwelt upon the sublime and beautiful others spoke continually of weeping and sorrow.

And the clergymen of our day speak according to their mental organism. Some of them are a hard-hearted race of men, for they speak continually of future torments. Others, more congenial, speak of the beauties of the universe and incomprehensible works of God. Some lead their congregations with a golden cord of love, others drive them with whips of scorpions. They all see by the same light and are animated by the same spirit. Where, then, is the great spiritual difference? Is it not in their mental organism? We see the same difference in their congregations. They are all taught by the same clergyman, attend the same church and claim the same reward.

Try them on a case of charity; some of them would not give the sunny side of a stump to a frozen beggar, others give even to the undeserving.

All of them do act according to their mental organism. Talk about the spirit! The character of the spirit is always determined by the material with which it comes in contact. A man is a good or a bad man upon the basis of his mental organism.

Behold the ancient pyramids of distant days; contemplate the magnificent temples of succeeding ages, and all the buildings erected for devotion. They stand as silent as the dead material of which they are composed. The human brain is the great spiritual temple of humanity. It is holy ground, consecrated by the unseen hand, upon which every mother in the world can rear the spiritual edifice of her children, though it be upon a puncheon floor inclosed with the rude logs of her native land.

Daniel said to Belshazzar, when he read the hand-writing on the wall: "Thou art weighed in the balances, and found wanting; thy kingdom is divided, and given to the Medes and Persians." No one believes that the king's body had been weighed in a pair of scales and found wanting in avoirdupois weight. The most refined results of the human mind have received a name, and that name is *honor*. The king's honor had been weighed and found wanting. Belshazzar was not a Jew, nor did he observe the Jewish ritual.

Now, I appeal to this assembly; you all have friends and associates, some of them you would trust with your money—you would trust them with your lives—others you would not trust with a pair of skates, because you have weighed their honor in your balances and found it wanting. The language of men, in their associations, rites, ceremonies and professions, in all ages or countries, perish or change form. But if they possess the principle of honor, it is imperishable. You may steal my money, burn my house and tarnish my goods; but, Oh God, save me from the dark assassin who would unjustly tarnish my honor!

Go with me to an ancient castle Its glory lies moldering in the dust—upon its features the hand of fate has dealt relentless ruin. The stream of time has left it away back in the dusky age. Slightly beneath the crumbling rubbish we find a coat; take it up, examine it, it may have been worn by the founder of the Chaldean empire or him who laid the foundation stone of a pyramid in Egypt. Stamped with the shape of humanity, we know it once covered a man; nothing more does it reveal—poor, poor, dumb garment.

Look! here is the man himself—or rather the body—wonderfully preserved from the fate of decay. The lips are beautiful as ever.—Speak! tell thy ancient rights and fervent prayers—they are as silent as the senseless rubbish clustered 'round their moldering form; whatever sounds they may have once uttered, whatever words they may have once spoken, like the coat the body was nothing but the garment that covered the true seed of honor.

One more picture and the curtain falls.

The pictures of the men of progress, put in a frame

together, are being hung up in our parlors. "But," says one, "that is Infidelity—better preserve the pictures of the holy mefi of old." That is the individuality of poor human nature, that said morality is dead without religion—it is the same man who said there is a conflict between science and revelation.

There is no conflict between true science and true revelation. Any problem that does not prove itself is no science. Twice two are four—figures are a science because they prove themselves. Astronomy demonstrates the course of the planets, and their contact in eclipse one with another before it takes place; and geology, and all other sciences worthy of the name, prove themselves. And what is revelation? There is no power in the universe that can reveal ignorance. To reveal is to uncover, to make known, to give the light of knowledge; and anything that is not made known is not revealed.

Standing under the mantle of charity, we witness a great conflict of human faith—and no wonder, faith is not a science or revelation. Faith is a feature of education, and applies only to conditions—for all nations agree to the great problem of a future life. The spirit of liberty guarantees to every man his own faith. It is a pure philanthrophy and a noble philosophy that consecrates every man's faith upon the altar of Charity, a beautiful and blindfolded goddess, who is bearing millions of our race, of all nations and countries, on the wide wings of hope, to eternity in a local spot; a heaven adorned with precious stones and paved with gold; a babyhouse of the soul of ignorance and picture of the dark ages.

I endeavored, in my lecture on Time and Motion, to unfold the infinity of the universe, space without limit, worlds without end. Time and motion belong to the planets, the planets belong to space. God and eternity are everywhere. The spirit of intellect pervades the universe, and animates the soul of man here, hereafter and forever. It does not enter the tomb—the grave, and all the powers of darkness, do not bind it. The armies of death perish at its feet. It survives the revolution of planets and the wreck of worlds; pervades the incomprehensible circle of space intwined in the arms of destiny.

GENIUS AND POETRY.

GENIUS.

[In ancient fable an old man of venerable aspect and silver beard, unlike other heathen gods, he ruled no particular passion or element, but loaned a helping hand to all, the Poet, Author, Architect, Teacher, Navigator, Statesman, Orator, Theologian, General in the field and all others, even in the simplest avocations of life may consult him to advantage.]

He lives not in a sealed house,
He dwells in the open air,
He is not found in robes of wealth,
Neither bound up in classic schools.

He lives in the wind, and rides on the breeze
Dwells in the forest and tenants the trees.

O! tell me where and when
True Genius comes to men?

In easy seat or cushion chair,
He never comes to hear your prayer.

In ease of body or of mind,
No mortal can true Genius find.
Faithful to all—and ever true—
Work, work! and he will work with you;
Work at what you can truly do,
And he will come and work with you.
His art is work, his heart is brave,
He loves the free, and hates the slave,
He lives with all who soar above—
Pure as light, and gentle as love.

MY NATIVE LAND.

ADDRESSED TO YOUNG AMERICA.

In ages past—almost obscure,
We trace the germs of liberty,
For ancient Greece in days of yore,
Emerging from obscurity,
Gave birth to men who lived to love,
And all their love was liberty.
Crushed to earth by tyrant heel,
Long ages slept in lethargy,
Aroused to meet the foeman's steel,
And in the name of liberty,
Fought fresh battles on the field
Of young and brave America.
Our fathers fought and bravely died,
When death would pay off tyranny;
They met the foemen side by side,
And fought to win our liberty.
The grateful heart adores the name
They won for their posterity;
On land, on sea 'tis all the same,
The watchword is "Our Liberty."
For teeming lands and homes made dear,
By all the ties of purity,
They held the claim without a fear,
And still they fought for liberty.
With their brave blood, as pure as light,
And free from the germs of tyranny,
The last brave call heard in the fight,
Was, leave to us "Our Liberty."
A playful boy accosted me,
With words of wisdom—I may say,

For lads that climb an apple tree,
His name was Young America.
With golden locks and ruddy cheeks,
He spoke in plaintive tones, so mild,
The loving heart must ever seek,
The memory of the growing child.
In every State, so broad and fair,
The little boys triumphant stand,
And I must tell you, that they are
The glory of my native land.
He spoke of Congress, and the men
Who represent the present age,
The heroes of the sword and pen,
The soldier, and the stately sage.
He spoke of time, long in the past,
When clubs and sticks were used by men,
But now we travel on so fast,
We only need to use the pen.
He spoke of Justice, with her scales
Suspended from her legal hand,
Stamped on my heart, with plaintive tales,
The glory of my native land.
He spoke of all our history past,
And then he wav'd his little hand;
I saw in him—from first to last,
The glory of my native land.
His name is one—to all the same,
He stood where all the boys must stand,
And to the busy world proclaim
The glory of their native land.

To him I spoke, in kind and loving words,
Roam through the woods and hear the singing birds,
Be just to all, and ever justice love,

Steal not the sweet little eggs of a dove.
Be just to birds, for justice first began
In the wild woods, with primitive man;
Be bold in thought, be bold in action too,
Be bold in justice, and in virtue true.
Be true to thyself, be just when you pray,
As just in the week as on the Lord's day;
Of all the problems ponder'd o'er so long,
It is the living test of right and wrong.
Boys who never steal an egg, or drink a dram,
Make men who never swindle Uncle Sam.
A flower planted in the youthful mind,
Full-blown manhood never fails to find.
The stings of wrong, that with the boy began,
Will follow up his growth and sting the man.
Then with a gentle pressure of the hand,
Casting o'er the broad and beautiful land.
The old, the honest are passing swiftly away,
The men of the future are the boys of to-day.
The learn'd, and the wise, the good and the brave.
Are passing away and filling the grave.
If examples were blank, no mortal could see,
What the rising generation would be.
Men make boys, and boys make men, *good* or *bad*,
The mold is cast—and finished with the lad.
This great country—hills and plains, lakes and boys,
Iron arms, long rivers, its hopes and joys;
From sea to sea, beneath a genial sun,
Great in extent, in union, one.
For you the struggling past has lived to save,
The land of the free, and home of the brave.
To you transmitted with a generous hand,
Treasures of a broad and beautiful land,
And you with a fond helpmate by your side,

May blend sweet home with a national pride.
The rivers, and lakes, the towns, and the lands,
Will soon be transmitted to your hands;
The sacred records, and government too,
Will also be transmitted to you.
Old fate is coming with her magic wand,
Peering all through this beautiful land,
And whether in search of the sword or the pen,
Will seldom mistake representative men.
Be just, and true, and never be too late,
Having no fears of fortune, or of fate;
Work for the right and never be afraid,
The right is at par, and is always paid.
Work with the brain, and work with the hand,
Work for the right, work for your native land.
Live with the just, and die with the brave,
And flowers of fame will bloom o'er your grave.
Think for yourself—mold your thought refined,
Treasure in the brain jewels of the mind;
For men have thought before, and thought sublime,
Through all the busy world before your time;
Unfolded worlds from Diamonds in the sky,
Scan'd endless space with artificial eye.
Gave life to words, and talk'd across the sea,
Released the slave, the human mind is free,
Free to think in every shape, and form,
To raise the wind and to calm the storm.

RISE AND FALL OF OLD NICK.

ADDRESSED TO THE DEVIL.

Come Beelzebub, thou sneaking ape of time,
Conceived in sin, and born in open crime;
Transgressing the law—long years ago,
The charges are made, stern justice must know,
What pleadings are brought to lie in the court,
Guilty, or not guilty you must report.
The judges are waiting, anxious to know,
What you will plead, with whom you will go.
Come honestly up and answer the suit,
Charged with tasting forbidden fruit;
You fled from the garden—in shape a snake,
Determined to capture all you could take.
Afraid of the light, slip'd through the dark,
Crossed over the flood, outside of the ark;
Afflicted old Job, and strip'd of his wealth,
Entered his flesh and poisoned his health.
From the land of Uz you followed the Jews,
From tribe to tribe you carried the news,
Stood at the altar, and wrote with the Scribes,
To the king of Persia you gave ten tribes.
Grew handsomely large, and strong by degrees,
Your form was changed by the Pharisees.
In Babylonian captivity—
Your serpent form lack'd activity,
The Pharisees first gave you legs and feet,
With dragon head they made your form complete.
To travel 'round the world, o'er hill and bog,
Followed by the three-headed Grecian dog.
Then with Jew and Greek, sneaking through the land,
To show the wicked world how Devils stand,

Deceiving them all with wonderful ease
By scouting the faith of the Sadducees.
Then tempting the Good, for forty long days,
Threw up the sponge, and spoke in his praise.
Rebuked by the Good, you enter'd the swine,
Persuading some men to root in that line.
Last seen by Michael, as he supposes,
Claiming the bones and body of Moses.
Next seen by St. John, revealing your reign,
Lamenting your fate, and bound with a chain,
Accused by the just, and judged by your peers,
Was banished from the Jews a thousand years.
Forsaking these men, and leaving their home,
Prospected with Greeks—and settled at Rome,
Spread with the faithful all over the grove,
Stripping all men as you stripped old Job.
The charges in short, summed up in brief,
All men call you a liar and a thief.
With charges so grave, and granted fair play,
In defense of yourself, what can you say?
The Devil rose up, and shaking his mane,
Opened his mouth in eloquent strain,
With sparks in his eyes, and tongue rolling 'round,
With feet wide apart, and tail on the ground,
Rattled his hoofs, no longer a snake,
Hell-d up his head, and boldly he spake—
"As thin as the air, and still as the grave,
I live with the bad, and work with the knave,
Molding the mean, and greeting the grand,
I'm passing through each house in the land,
Forsaking the wise, I stay with the fool,
No charges are made, I keep a free school,
Eat without bread, and fatten on a fuss,
Abandon the dead, as useless to us—

The living are mine, and all I can get,
Are handsomely taken in their own net.
My traps are set, both early and late,
Credulous game is caught without bait.
The field is broad, and wide as the earth—
To credulous game, all classes give birth.
I'm sure to be sought, by the mean and low,
The rich and the proud will come to the show.
In castle and cot, the great and the small,
Aside from the light, will give me a call.
Bad men follow me, wherever I go—
Begging me out of all that I know,
My thoughts are quick, and given at a stroke,
Are easy to learn when under the yoke,
Coasting the sea, and all over the land,
I meet with men to take by the hand,
Restless and rude, for I never was kind,
Though lost to the good, I'm not hard to find.
I pass by the good, the just I abhor,
Have constantly kept all nations at war.
Have wrote with the learn'd, embellished the pages
By stratagems sought—have darken'd all ages,
Have bound to the stake, and hung with the rope,
Slept with the queen, and dined with the Pope,
Familiar with abuse and lost to all shame,
Hopeless of life, *I am nothing but a name.*
A wonderful name, all over the earth,
The passions of men, have given me birth,
The passions are good, when properly used,
The Devil comes in to see them abused.
When passions are found, the force of the mind,
The Devil himself, you never will find.
Remember these words, a wise man said,

'The Devil is not in a good man's head,'
I'm vanishing now, out of your sight,
Gentlemen *all*, I bid you good night."

THE CONFEDERATE FLAG.

[The following poetic address was preserved by a rebel woman, and is inserted for the benefit of those who did not witness the war spirit in Missouri in 1861. The rebel ladies of Plattsburg manufactured a very fine confederate flag, intended for the company of Captain Crumlow, who were upon the eve of starting to join the army of General Sterling Price. A formal presentation was arranged—the company and a large number of citizens assembled at the Plattsburg College. A person whose name and address was not preserved, presented the flag in the name of the ladies. Captain Crumlow requested your orator to receive the flag in behalf of the company with a suitable response. Your orator received the flag, and holding it in his right hand, partly unfurled, returned the following response :}

LADIES.

Should blood and carnage fill the land,
And cities and towns no longer stand;
Should conquer'd courage gasp for breath,
And your defenders, lie cold in death—
Butcher'd and mangled on the field,
No arm be left, this banner to shield;
Take up its folds, with tender hands,
And on the ground where virtue stands,
Trust in God, and consecrate
This banner to their mortal fate.
But, no such scene will ever stain
The coral of the human brain.
Mars may forge infernal rods,

And Northmen dream of *coal black gods;*
These lords will fail to come to time,
For Northmen in a southern clime.
Our country lies, both far and wide,
And in it dwells a native pride
No hand can conquer or subdue,
While held by such a brace as you.
In Crumlow's men you place your trust—
They'll bear this flag above the dust.

As the flag was handed to the standard-bearer of the company, Gen. D. R. Atchison, Ex-Senator of the United States, appeared on the stage to congratulate the speaker. Citizens threw up their hats, and ladies waved their 'kerchiefs in applause, while the company marched off with the banner thrown to the breeze, followed by running boys and idle negroes. A picture fitly representing the *brave heroism* with which Price's army went through the first year of the war.

FAMILY AND FATE.

ADDRESS TO A FEMALE RELATION.

You must not think the cares of life with me
Are smooth, and placid as a summer sea.
The joyous days, one by one revealed,
Turn fresh trouble long, long concealed·
Gray locks of time adorn the aching brow,
Unfinished work drags heavy now.

While on we march, in one continuous flood,
I'm but a drop of the commingled blood;
Homogeneous with the family name,

Preserving kindred ties and family fame;
So long, slowly wise and darkly great,
No stores of wit or large estate
To deck their graves or write their fate.

Meekly have I lived, and with the poor must die,
No stone to mark the ground where I must lie;
Sunk with the motley herd of human kind,
No trace that once I lived to leave behind;
A mound of earth alone remains with me—
'Tis all I ask, and all the proud can be.

When time shall cool my blood and steal my breath,
When life shall reach the silent shade of death,
When the cold, damp clods cluster 'round my head,
Earth to earth, sweet sister, will I be dead?
In this dark dream of death's long silent sleep,
I pray my niece these hopeful lines to keep.
Poor tired soul, humble and forgiving,
Without future hope, life ain't worth living.
Death is but a name magnified by fear,
The living elements that disappear
With nature's soft hand, are forever here.
In these elements the hope of heaven,
A living hope by kind nature given.

Come, genius, come, tune thy living song
To 'muse the merry world while I sleep so long;
Sleep not with me—act with the living throng;
Cheer up sad times with merry heart and head—
Lie not entombed, but resurrect the dead.

Dark mantled fear, with his bow and quiver,
Stands on the brink of death's dark river;
The shield of antiquity covers his head—
He shoots at the living, not at the dead;

Through trembling *faith* his fleeting arrows run,
Inflicting a thousand deaths instead of one.
When in future bliss, or in hopeful prayer,
No mortal ken can see just what we are.

God gives the mind to us as free as air;
Life lies in action and is everywhere;
Above, below, around, through endless space,
Life, mind and light fill every friendly place.
Darkness and death, obscure to human sight,
Can only remain where there is no light.
Life, mind and light, eternal in the skies,
Solace of the weak and soul of the wise—
Light never was dark, and life never dies,

Through endless space the thoughtful man can pierce,
Untarnished mind pervades the universe.
Shall the dark, silent tomb, with bolts and bars,
Imprison mind that travels through the stars?
Shall ponderous matter, nature's body, find
Dominion over active, thinking mind?
Men do not perish with their flesh and bones,
Or cease to be, when they have ceased their groans.
For flesh and bones are not the man defined—
Strange elements of a different kind,
Reveal the man as they reveal the mind.

The brain is not the mind, as some suppose;
We see it there, but know not where it goes.
Spirit, soul, apparition, thought refined,
High, deep, quick, endless—Oh God! what is mind?
It moves my hand, molds my measured verse,
Moves everything, pervades the universe.

TWILIGHT.

INTERMEDIATE BODY AND SOUL.

The rainbow hooped the eastern sky,
The melting clouds passed softly by,
The sun had sunk behind the trees—
Twilight hung on the western breeze.
The earth rolled on with day and night;
But who shall claim the soft twilight?
Retreating light, cast on the ground,
Made cottage-homes a scene profound.
The plowman left his furrowed field,
The light of day just half concealed.
The house-wife spread her generous board,
Received her mate and blessed the Lord.
The rivers waved in calm delight
Beneath the silent shades of night;
Spirits, concealed by grave-yard stones,
Silently sleep with dead men's bones;
The moving earth dark robes unfurled,
And sleep subdued just half the world;
The iron tongue of time had told
That dreary night was growing old;
Aurora ope'd her wakeful eye,
Twilight dawned in the eastern sky;
The day of life must also close,
The night of death no mortal knows;
Let all men view in calm delight
The evening shade of life's twilight,
When full of years and honors too,
The evening brings solace to you;
Departing day will bid farewell,
When twilight comes no tongue can tell—

So, calm and thoughtful, let us see
What twilight brings to you and me;
A scene behind and one before—
Between two worlds, Oh! mind explore
Boundless realms and endless space,
See time and fate stand face to face.
The night of death, so cold and dark,
The faith we have is but a spark
Of living light in every breast,
The rich and poor will all be blest.
The busy day of human life,
When time is full of peace and strife,
With scenes behind and hope before,
The rich forget the needy poor.
Beyond the earth no poor are found,
If there we tread on holy ground,
The poor are rich, the good are great,
In coming to the future state.
When twilight comes the sun has set,
The earth recedes, and we have met
Where light and shade obscure the sight,
'Twixt life and death we see twilight.

THE DEVIL AND TOM WALKER.

Kentucky, the home of Clay, Crittenden, Marshall, Prentice, and other men of distinction, was also the home of one Thomas Walker, who, by circumstances and the trials of the times, gave his name to history. Living near Frankford, it was in that city, that he appeared as a hero, playing the fiddle and drinking whisky.

Tom was well advanced in years, when the Rev. William Miller, from a close scrutiny of the prophecies of the Old Testament, predicted the end of the world in 1843. Whatever may have been Tom's good or bad qualities, he was a confirmed Millerite. One day in Frankford, as the dissolution drew near, Tom to drown fear, indulged immoderately in intoxicating drinks, and while he was in a stupefied and senseless condition, a party of Frankford boys, from eight to twelve years of age, just emerging into the bright paths of youth, and of course, heedless of the approaching dissolution of the globe ; had by some means obtained possession of a large *raw hide*. Upon this they carefully placed Tom's body and carried it to the suburbs of the city, and there stretching Tom upon the ground, carefully covered him with the *raw hide*, and then placing upon him a large pile of straw set it on fire.

In the meantime, Tom had dreamt the world was ended, and himself arrived in the infernal regions. The heat of the fire had aroused Tom from his lethargy, imagination completed the picture, and Tom rushing out from the flames, with burning straw streaming from his person, cried at the top of his voice: "The Devil and Tom Walker." From this circumstance "The Devil and Tom Walker," became a by-word or slang phrase in Kentucky. Tom afterward joined a temperance society and became a *sober man*.

In the following poem he is chosen to personate temperance and virtue, while the Devil personates vice and crime.

The Devil and Tom Walker one afternoon,
    A solemn subject profoundly discussed;
The Devil was anxious to keep a saloon,
    If to him, his grace could honestly trust.
Tom Walker affirmed, " the business was bad."
    The Devil stood up and curtly replied :
"Idle men everywhere, would surely be glad,
    If the business could be honestly tried."
Tom Walker said : " The history of the past,
    Recorded saloons, as they have bursted,
A notable thing from first to last—
    Honesty, has always been worsted."
"A necessary evil," said the Devil,
    "In every age, and in every clime ;

Therefore bad men can surely be civil,
   When dissembling will cover a crime."
Tom Walker said: "Vice is not necessary,
   Though Spirits and Demons may pretend—
To mix them up from June to January,
   Their vice and virtue never will blind.
That evils are necessary, some have told,
   Inducing the thoughtless to believe;
Because the problem is ancient, and old,
   And well calculated to deceive."
The Devil conceded the point to Tom,
   But said to himself: "The will is the way,
The club-house will gather some custom,
   And in it, I can gather some pay.
Idle men drink, and idle men fight,
   Idle men fuss, and idle men tight—
Sleep through the day, and fuss all night.
   Virtue may fade, but the dollar is bright,
Eyes go blind, when the dollar's in sight.
   Vice lives in the dark, and flees from the light,
Gives virtue the dodge, and justice the blight;
   If Tom is wrong, the Devil is right."
Changing his tone, the Devil contended;
   "Bad men love justice as well as the good,
And justice will swear they have defended,
   The cause of the bad as well as the good."
"You argue your case exceedingly well,
   Guarding the points, to meet Tom Walker·
Carry some justice to the gates of hell,
   To hear the sound of a smooth talker."
"Older than the State, stronger than the wise,
   You live at the root of the government;
True men everywhere must open their eyes,
   Or quietly suffer the punishment."

"Ashamed of your trade, you live in the dark,
　Borrow the cloak of some other game;
Put on the dog make other trades bark,
　Sounding your business in some other name."
"The patriarch Noah planted the vine,
　His household joined to gather the grape;
He also drank his fill of the wine,
　If the Devil caught Noah, who can escape?"
Tom Walker may plead, and Tom may talk,
　The Devil takes notes to feather his nest,
Can silently go, where Tom can't walk,
　Give two in the game and play for the rest.
The Devil has played for long ages past,
　A winning game on all classes of men;
Detected by Tom, checkmated at last,
　By subscribing his game with ink and pen.
Who, like the Devil would ruin the right,
　By blighting the young with still-worm food?
Live in the dark, and darken the light,
　Drink lager beer and call the stuff good.
How darker than dreary night it is,
　To all who drink destructive wine;
The Devil is sure to claim for his,
　The sunny side of virtue's line.
Tom Walker lived to see the vision end,
　Through burning straw an awful sight;
The Devil to him a faithless friend,
　And all who live to learn him right.
Shades of the dead and the Devil's dark light,
　Tom Walker no more, nor Devil in sight;
Cut loose from the wine, and never get tight.
　Ladies and Gentlemen good night—good night!

THE BEAUTIFUL SNOW.

AN EMBLEM OF VIRTUE.

Rainbow of thought, in the poet's soft eye,
Encircle the mind with beautiful sky;
To speak of the pure virtues of earth,
The beautiful thoughts, emblems give birth.
Nothing on earth that's treasur'd below
Is half so pure as beautiful snow.

God clothed the earth with air and water,
Eve, the first fair and beautiful daughter,
Transmitted to her descending race
Angelic form, and beautiful face;
And purity too, each gallant should know,
As pure and stainless as beautiful snow.

Let me say to each descending daughter,
Cling to the emblem of air and water;
God save the daughter, pure and fair,
Beauty, blended with water and air,
The treasures of earth honored below
Girls are as pure as beautiful snow.

Let nature's demands defiantly hold
Sinful indulgence, and offers of gold.
Sensitive as the blushing young daughter
Are flowers of spring sighing for water;
Sin's dark hand slightly touch'd will show,
Corruption's mark in beautiful snow.

The power of state or pride of sage
In all of the past, or a future age,
Will never surpass the emblem so fair,
Made by the blending of water and air;

No treasure on earth that woman can show
Will capture the heart like beautiful snow.

The love of display and treasures of gold
In markets of shame, where virtue is sold.
Worthless emblem, Oh! beautiful daughter,
Cling to the emblem of air and water
Cast in your bosom, in order to show,
Your purity, like the beautiful snow.

Wisdom's bright eye may delinquently trace
The lines of the form, and beauties of face;
Perfection may claim, that nature has made
A blushing young rose in beautiful shade;
As worthless as chaff the daughter may go,
Whose virtue's not like beautiful snow.

Cast in the dark by a fatal mistake,
From beautiful snow no mortal can take,
The stain of the crime, and leave you as fair
As the emblem made of water and air.
Beautiful daughter, as onward you go,
Always remember the beautiful snow.

BEAUTIFUL SNOW.

The following, beautiful poem, was written by a woman in St. Louis many years ago, and was published in the newspapers at the time. From it your orator received the idea of writing "The Beautiful Snow." Thinking the *old poem* worthy of preservation, it is here printed in its original form.

Oh, the snow, the beautiful snow,
Filling the sky and the earth below:

Over the house-top, over the street,
Over the heads of the people you meet,
    Dancing,
      Flirting,
        Skimming along,
Beautiful snow, it can do nothing wrong;
Flying to kiss a fair lady's cheek,
Clinging to lips in a frolicsome freak;
Beautiful snow from the heaven above,
Pure as an angel, gentle as love.

Oh, the snow, the beautiful snow,
How the flakes gather and laugh as they go
Whirling about in their maddening fun—
It plays in its glee with every one—
    Chasing,
      Laughing,
        Hurrying by,
It lights on the face, and it sparkles the eye,
And the dogs, with a bark and a bound,
Snap at the crystals that eddy around—
The town is alive and its heart is aglow,
To welcome the coming of beautiful snow.

How widely the crowd goes swaying along,
Hailing each other with humor and song;
How the gay sledges like meteors flash by,
Bright for a moment, then lost to the eye;
    Ringing,
      Swinging,
        Dashing they go,
Over the crust of the beautiful snow—
Snow so pure when it falls from the sky,
As to make one regret to see it lie

To be trampled and tracked by thousands of feet,
Till it blends with the filth in the horrible street.

Once I was as pure as the snow, but I fell—
Fell like the snowflakes from heaven to hell;
Fell to be trampled as filth in the street;
Fell to be scoffed, to be spit on and beat;
   Pleading,
     Cursing,
        Dreading to die,
Selling my soul to whosoever would buy;
Dealing in shame for a morsel of bread;
Hating the living, fearing the dead.
Merciful God! Have I fallen so low?
And yet I was once like the beautiful snow!
Once I was fair as the beautiful snow,
With an eye like a crystal, a heart like its glow;
Once I was loved for my innocent grace—
Flattered and sought for the charms of my face.
   Father,
     Mother,
       Sister, all,
God and myself I have lost by my fall;
The veriest wretch that goes shivering by,
Will make a wide swoop lest I wander too nigh;
For all that is on or above me, I know
There's nothing that's pure as the beautiful snow.
How strange it should be that this beautiful snow
Should fall on a sinner with nowhere to go!
How strange should it be when night comes again!
If the snow and the ice struck my desperate brain!
   Fainting,
     Freezing,
       Dying alone,

Too wicked for prayer, too weak for a moan
To be heard in the streets of the crazy town,
Gone mad in the joy of the snow coming down;
To be and to die in my terrible woe,
With a bed and a shroud of the beautiful snow.

Helpless and foul as the trampled snow,
Sinner, despair not, Christ stoopeth low
To rescue the soul that is lost in its sin,
And raise it to life and enjoyment again.
    Groaning,
      Bleeding,
        Dying for thee,
The Crucified hung on the accursed tree;
His accents of mercy fell soft on thine ear—
Is there mercy for me? Will he hear my prayer?
Oh! God! in the stream that for sinners did flow,
Wash me, and I shall be whiter than snow.

THE WORKMAN'S SATURDAY NIGHT.

A TRIBUTE TO HONEST LABOR.

Through the wide world 'tis cheerful delight,
To speak of life scenes on Saturday night,
When merry workmen and their wages meet,
And leave the cold shop for the homeward street,
To see the dark mantle cover the sky—
The light in the cottage meeting his eye;
The patient inmates expecting him back
To replenish the house with all they lack.
The busy housewife preparing his food,
And scraping the scraps to make the *grub good*.

A prattling boy, some four years old or more,
With arms extended meets him at the door;
The little eyes turn'd up so clear and fair,
Says, "Papa, baby climbed up by the chair."
His hopes tell his fears like the Jewish Dan,
That his baby boy will soon be a man.
His wife scans the scene, delighted to know
That all through the house, the baby's the show
That mothers must think their babies a show,
And workmen thus feel—pray, how do you know?
God trusted me with a bright baby boy,
Who taught me to feel his babyhood joy.
If God gave you the same little treasure;
He also gave the same baby-measure.
No measure so pure to measure delight,
As baby pleasures on Saturday night.
His mission on earth and love of his life,
Is blended at home with children and wife.
His purse in her pocket—rich as a Jew,
Replenish the house, I trust it to you;
The ends made to meet in a workman's life,
By none so even as a truthful wife.
Let the public halls go on in grand display,
And workmen go home where they love to stay.
Let the tempter come, with allurements bold,
That Madam Rumor's tongue has *softly told*,
Enticing stories of high standing fame,
That price the state below the promised name.
Let all the scenes darting through the mind,
Leave labor's love and workingmen behind.
Flora's fair fields, adorned with bright flowers,
Can ne'er win the heart from his cottage hours.
Home and his children, the hope of his life,
No vision so clear as love for his wife.

The fame of the great ne'er made a measure
Large enough to hold *cottage-bound pleasure*
He works with his hands and then takes his rest
In the bosom of love—God of the blest.
Come, fashion and frolic, blooming and bright,
But leave to brave workmen *Saturday night*.

INSIDE VIEW OF THE UNITED STATES MAIL

REVEALED BY THE ANGEL OF OBSERVATION.

Letter No. 1.

Going West will give each man a farm,
And living West will do the East no harm,
As people spread along the Western shore,
The Eastern man will find an open door.
The blue bird laid in the di-dapper's nest,
And the golden eggs are found in the West.
—Land Agent.

Letter No. 2.

Katy's sick and Jennie's gone to school,
The storm is over and the weather's cool,
Brother Tom's married and his wife is gay
She's too fast for him, so the people say
Some awful things, I never ought to speak.
Remember this, I'm coming home next week.
—Confidential Sister.

Letter No. 3.

The note was protested, won't go in bank,
And you are requested to sign this blank.

The current house has failed—aint worth a cent,
Long trust ran off and didn't pay his rent.
Horn'd by the bulls and squeezed by the bears,
The golden-wing gods demand our prayers.
     —FAILING MERCHANT.

Letter No. 4.

The little kitten's dead, I'm so distressed,
To keep my spirits up I do my best.
Come home right son, I'm so very sad,
When I see Tom, O, I-l-e be so glad!
     —AFFECTIONATE LITTLE SISTER.

Letter No. 5.

I thought so Betsey, when you married Jim,
The devil a bit would I take from him.
To live in a fuss folks never oughter,
But prove yourself to be *mother's daughter.*
To fight and scratch is surely a sin,
But when he starts the fuss al'ys go in.
     —MOTHER-IN-LAW.

Letter No. 6.

I-v-e bought some land, paid half the money down,
Inclosed y-o-u-'l-l find a note on Billy Brown.
Collect it right away. Tell him I-l-e *sue.*
Pay Joe the *coin,* I-l-e pay the church for *you.*
     —CHURCH MEMBER.

Letter No. 7.

Come over here, Rip, the best place I-v-e seen,
Lots of boys in town, and half of 'em green.
I played last night till four. Won all the stakes.
Bacchus among us with boots full o' snakes.

Morpheus embraced me till the clock struck ten,
Ate a late breakfast, looked 'round me, and then
Acted *agent* through the day, softly and wise,
Till watchmen on duty all shut their eyes.
And t-h-e-n the foolish boys go in, y-o-u b-e-t.
Come over here, Rip, and help spread the *net*.
—Fast Young Man.

Letter No. 8.

The case is lost. The witness on the stand
Did not remember the lines of the land.
His mind was short, I told you it would be,
The cost is on y-o-u, the work was on me.
—Attorney at Law.

Letter No. 9.

Silly went to York, and there she caught a beau.
He came home with *her*, a *silly* chap you *know*.
Silly is so strange, as ugly as old sin,
But when she meets a beau she always takes him in.
Jenny do come home, sweet Kitty Hope is dead,
And Hopeful wants to know who will make his bread.
—Old Maid.

Letter No. 10.

Old dad is dead, I want to break the will.
Joe gets the stock, the farm's left to Bill.
Non compos mentis, I think is the plea.
If learned in the law, stern justice could see,
That fruit is the same grown on the same tree.
I left old dad but nineteen years ago;
Nobody nursed him but Billy and Joe;
To feel the soft side they never were lazy,
And thus by degrees run the old man crazy.

I depend on y-o-u, how much will it take?
I'm willin' to pay if the will will break.
—PRODIGAL SON.

Letter No. 11.

If I could sell the world I'd make it cheap,
A ten-cent mark upon each world I'd keep,
To show the *world* I sell the world *low down;*
I'd sell to every man that comes to town
Wholesale supplies. I'd buy from endless space,
At the low price of half a cent apiece.
The foolish merchant fails for want of eyes
To scan surrounding space for cheap supplies.
—CHEAP JOHN.

Letter No. 12.

I read eleven letters *just to see*
What a wonderful thing the mail would be
Turned inside out by the *Good Angel's* hand,
And read to all the people in the land.
The different thoughts of the human race,
Brought to open light and face to face.
How variegated ever and anon
To read the statesman and reveal the crown;
The ever playful, prattling pedagogue;
The cunning, deep-designing demagogue;
The love-sick girl, the widow and the maid;
And what the tearful, weeping wife has said.
The *Good Angel* knows what measure belongs
To artless prose and warm poetic songs;
To fill the tearless eye to overflow,
And teach the heart to feel another's woe.
The *Good Angel* reveals so very slow,
The indulgent reader must surely know,

To turn the ponderous mail inside out,
A year of holidays must come about.
Pardon me now, and in the future look
To the *Good Angel* for another book.
    —THE ANGEL OF OBSERVATION.

HARD TIMES.

Come, hopeful men, I am prepared
To tell you why the times are hard.
Around the world, go where you will,
Across the plain and o'er the hill,
To labor for the needful dimes,
You meet the cry of cold hard times.
Nothing can be without a cause,
Hard-times are made by certain laws;
Individual action brings
Hard-times to people and to kings.
The poor girl strives to ape the rich,
Pays a fancy price for every stitch.
Her father works with all his skill
For extra dimes to pay the bill.
The poor boy thinks hard work *a shame*,
Without a fortune or a name,
Will try to make himself a man
By joining hands with some *low clan*.
The farmer works to clear the woods;
The merchant sells him shoddy goods.
The doctor gives his poison pills,
The patients die or pay the bills.
Less work is done for want of hands

To clear the ground or till the lands.
The lawyer pleads his client's case—
Travels 'round from place to place,
Relates his plea in open court.
The judge rules out his last report.
New bondsmen come to stop the fight,
And leave him where the wool-is-tight.
True justice is so far away,
The poor, to wait the law's delay,
Must try to do without their dues,
And tread the way without their shoes.
Another class of men, 'tis true,
Pretended friends of me and you,
Some millions, more or less, I think.
Who say the world was made to drink.
They drink *bad health* to one another,
Each pulls down a falling brother;
Deplete the State to pay their crimes,
Disguise the truth and cry hard-times.
Rum and fashion, pride and folly,
Jim and John and Cousin Molly,
Fostering all these foolish crimes,
Must ever make cold hard-times.
No statesman, but an humble bard,
Has told you why the times are hard.
Let every one their mission fill,
Pay off your debt and stop the still,
Train up the young as they should go,
Let old and young their duty know,
Earn before you spend your dimes,
And then, we won't have hard-times.

THE POWER OF TRUTH.

O virtuous truth! on my tongue repose,
Like dew from heaven on the blushing rose;
A healing balm for every wind that blows;
Star of the morning—light of ev'ry age—
Prop of the beggar, and pride of the sage—
Solace of the weak—glory of the strong—
Guide of the critic and the poet's song;
Pure as the diamond, as brilliant and bright,
Tho' covered with falsehood dark as the night,
Will furnish the mind with a ray of light,
Tho' faint as the infant ray of the morn
Heralds the news that young day is born.
Sure as the heavenly-piercing eye of day,
Peeps e'er the hills, to look dark night away,
Ungarnished truth will banish falsehood.

THE WHEELS OF TIME.

How slow the iron wheels of Time can turn,
When from the hidden future we would learn
Some anxious lesson of eventful life!
How slow, how deadly slow, and with what strife,
They seem to turn upon the road of Time;
How harsh upon the ear their sound doth chime!
But when the dark-faced future holds in store
Some reckoning of a different score—
Some fearful lesson that we have to learn—
How swift the nimble wheels of Time can turn!

THE DAYS OF MY CHILDHOOD.

I am wand'ring back to the days of my childhood—
The mill, the pasture, and deep tangled wildwood;
The orchard, the cellar, and apple that mellows,
The sound of the horn, and laugh of my fellows.
The morning's brief meal, and refreshments at noon,
The stroll in the wood by the light of the moon;
The bath in the river, and fisherman's line,
The herding of cattle, and feeding of swine.
The morning in the field, the song of the lark,
The evening at the cot, and play at the park;
The long nights of winter, and games of the season,
The fine flow of spirits ne'er tainted with treason.
The bright days of summer joyfully seen,
The rove through the garden of flowers serene;
The blossoms of spring, and the leaves of the fall,
The sound of the voice of a playmate's call;
The memories of childhood and young dreams of age
Are twin-sister flowers in the mind of the sage.
O sweet path of childhood, flowers of the past!
I traverse thee in dreams, and hug thee so fast!
When day opens eyes, and morning lays cold,
The gray hairs of age, and sorrows of old,
I would go back to slumber, live o'er again
The joys of my youth, forgetting the pain
Of age, sorrows, perplexities, and strife,
That shade and darken the last end of life.

IDOLS AND IDEAS.

ESSAY ON JACOB AND LABAN.

Turn back in history, four thousand years,
At Laban's house a brilliant youth appears.
Young Jacob, in the ardor of his life,
Willing to serve seven years for a wife.
Rachel and Leah concerted a plan,
To blindfold cupid and catch the young man.
Rachel was pretty and modestly shy,
Leah, the eldest, was weak in the eye.
Jacob was faithful, honest and kind,
The image of Rachel first in his mind.
Seven years service completed the trade;
Leban gave Jacob the blushing young maid;
The wedding at night bewilder'd his head,
And daylight found old Leah in his bed.
The hand of Rachel must Jacob deplore,
For Laban demanded seven years more;
The service performed, at Laban's demand,
Jacob took Rachel, at last, by the hand.
Rachel and Leah bore sons and daughters.
Jacob cast cattle with rods and waters;
His wages is stock, and all that he got
Was each cattle-calf found marked with a spot.
Laban loved to mold his gods in metal;
Jacob fill'd the fields with spotted cattle.
Old Laban's fortune, with his cattle went,
And Jacob saw the face of discontent.
With wives, and herds, and servants at command,
He left the Laban house for his native land;
With horn and hoof, and whoop and halloo,
With some to lead and some to follow,

And crop the grass on distant sods.
Young Rachel stole old Laban's gods,
Bereft of cattle, and his daughters too,
Old Laban thought it idle to pursue,
In summing up the ends and odds,
The old man missed his idol gods,
And paddled on to overtake,
As he thought, the treacherous Jake.
Laban and Jake met face and face,
Each maintained a sacred place.
The god of Laban—an Idol;
The God of Jacob—an Idea.
And there they planted a lasting stone,
That each should let the other alone.
On the east, the Syrian hero stood,
On the west, Jacob gave himself to God.
In rolling on the human flood,
Some will turn back to Laban's blood.
A golden calf since Aaron's day,
Is all that some can preach and pray,
While some in *folly*, go to seed,
And make idols of Christian creed.
God is an idea in the mind,
Eternal with all human kind.
All idols are to represent,
And in value not worth a cent.

THE DYING DRUNKARD TO HIS SOUL.

Heaven forsaken—for *one sin*,
The soul set out, when wine set in.
A vision of light in the deep dark!
I see the still—a living spark;
Bewildered like a fallen star,
Oh, how I wonder what you are!

Then—it surpasses me to know
In endless space—where you will go;
Shut out from heaven by decree,
As a wandering refugee;
To wander on from shore to shore
And never find an open door.

Traveling on, without hope or home,
Through endless ages yet to come—
No time to plead, no place for prayer,
'Tis desolation everywhere.
Oh, heaven come! do tell me why,
The drunkard's soul can never die;

The Devil, for one sin *alone*,
Will never claim you as his own.
Lost! Oh, Bacchus—thou God of wine;
Look upon this poor soul of mine;
Ope' thy bubbling wine-bottle eye—
And *as it lives*, let thy mission die.

THE MONEYLESS MAN *vs.* MONEYLESS WOMAN.

The Moneyless Man was composed by Henry T. Stanten, of Maysville, Kentucky. It has been read on the stage in the city of London, and won the applause of thousands of England's gifted orators.

Is there no secret place on the face of the earth,
Where charity dwelleth, where virtue hath birth,
Where bosoms in mercy and kindness will heave,
And the poor and the wretched shall ask and receive.

Is there no place on earth where a knock from the poor
Will bring a kind angel to open the door?
Ah! search the wide world whenever you can,
There's no open door for the moneyless man.

Go, look in your hall, where chandelier's light
Drives off with its splendor the darkness of night;
Where the rich, hanging velvet in shadowy fold,
Sweeps gracefully down with its trimmings of gold,

And the mirrors of silver take up and renew,
In long, lighted vistas, the wildering view.
Go there in your patches, and find if you can,
A welcoming smile for the moneyless man!

Go, look in yon church of the cloud-reaching spire,
Which gives back to the sun the same look of red fire;
Where the arches and columns are gorgeous within,
And the walls seem as pure as a soul without sin.

Go down the long aisle—see the rich and the great,
In the pomp and the pride of their worldly estate;
Walk down in your patches and find if you can,
Who opens a pew to a moneyless man.

Go look to yon judge, in his dark, flowing gown,
With the scales wherein law weigheth equity down,
Where he frowns on the weak and smiles on the strong,
And punishes right, while he justifies wrong;

Where jurors their lips on the Bible have laid,
To render a verdict they've already made;
Go there in the court room, and find if you can,
Any law for the cause of a moneyless man!

Go look in yon banks, where Mammon has told
His hundreds and thousands of silver and gold;
Where safe from the hands of the starving and poor,
Lies pile upon pile of the glittering ore;

Walk up to the counter—ah! there you may stay,
Till your limbs grow old and your hair turns gray,
And you'll find at the banks no one of the clan
With money to loan to a moneyless man!

Then go to your hovel, no raven has fed
The wife who has suffered too long for her bread.
Kneel down by her pallet and kiss the death frost
From the lips of the angel you poverty lost;

Then turn, in your agony, upward to God,
And bless, while it smites you, the chastening rod;
And you'l find at the end of your life's little span,
There's a welcome above for a moneyless man.

THE MONEYLESS WOMAN

Was written by your orator after reading the "Moneyless Man," and first published in 1868.

In answer to all Mr. Stanten has said,
I'll speak a kind word for the moneyless maid.
There is one place on earth, where a knock from the poor,
Will bring a kind angel to open the door.

I've searched the wide world in open review,
From the three-legged stool to the fine cushion'd pew,
And found by the dint of a wonderful scan,
The only true mate of the moneyless man.

Come, Mr. Stanten, and I'll open the door,
And show you the angel, so meek and so poor.

The merchant with his silks and satins for sale,
May listen an hour to a frivolous tale,
Or talk for a day of his diamonds and pearls,
But has nothing to say to moneyless girls.

The doctor, with his pills, forceps and knife,
Hoarding up money; the cost of your life,
Will purchase a coach, more easy to ride,
But seldom escorts a moneyless bride.

The farmer with his fields blooming and green,
Will go to the church to see and be seen,
And often returns to his hoe and spade,
But **never** takes home a moneyless maid.

The preacher condemns the goods of this life,
As unworthy—both husband and wife,

Looking beyond them for all of his bliss,
Seldom unites with a moneyless miss.

The lawyer sums up the strength of his **fees**,
To court your favor, will get on his knees,
For money alone, will honor your name,
But never pays court to a moneyless dame.

The statesman expounds the laws for a bank,
Rough hews a platform and stands on a plank,
Surveys the country, and tells of its fate,
But never will choose a moneyless mate.

The soldier with his sword, detesting a foe,
So gallant on the field his colors to show,
So brave at the call of the drum and the fife,
Is too timid to take a moneyless wife.

The poet will sing the story of fame,
Give frivolous things a glorious name;
Sing for a friend, or sing for a foeman,
But has no song for a moneyless woman.

Now, Mr. Stanten, return to your muse,
And measure her *feet*, to see what you lose,
Inspire her brain, deny if you can,
I've found a true mate for *the moneyless man*.

NOTE—When these poems are spoken on the stage, by a gentleman and lady, the lady should adopt the name of the gentleman speaking, instead of Mr. Stanten's

THE POET.

A man of sorrow, all compact, of imagination full; whose fertile brain never drops the blossom.

Rhymers are plenty. Poets are like

TOM WATSON'S DEER.

In joyous early times and back-woods life,
A party went out to hunt, and camped
By a certain stream called Little Fork.
And with the rising of the morning sun,
Hunting deer they went, two by two, save Tom,
Who went alone and traversed the woods
The livelong day, and with the setting sun
Returned to camp. His comrades, lively sat,
In merry chat, around the burning coals.
Ah! what luck? said one, as Tom walked up.
Good luck, said Tom, I've killed a dozen deer.
Where? Where? Where? said all of them at once.
Two I hung on Pleasant Hill, hard by the
New-built church. Four I left on Roebuck Ridge
Right west of Potter's field, on live oak trees.
Five are strung in Greenwood swamp, 'long the shore,
And face the East, right on the public road.
And one I left on Little Fork, right at
The Bailey Ford; and Tom Watson sat down.
Bob and I straight have come, from Pleasant Hill,
Passed the new-built church, and saw no deer,
Said Bill. We, too, have come from Roebuck Ridge,
Passed 'round the Potter's field, and saw no deer,
Said Joe. And we have come from Greenwood swamp,
Along the public road, and saw no deer,
Said Sam and Q. Tom Watson looked sad,
And rising up, he said: I hunted down

The Little Fork; when near the Bailey Ford,
A big buck bounced up. I leveled down
My fowling piece and shot him through the head,
And hung him on a Sweet-gum tree, right at
The Bailey Ford. Just then, Cliff Carlo came
And said: I have hunted up and down
The Little Fork, and crossed the Bailey Ford.
Did you see Tom's deer? said all at once.
No, I saw no game. Then Tom, laughing, said:
I take my boasting back—but, sure as fate,
I crossed the creek right at the Bailey Ford,
And looked with all my eyes, and in the mud,
Hard by the shore—I saw the d——d thing's *track*.

Farewell to all, both great and small,
Who live upon this dirty ball;
Remember me—God bless you all,
And *softly* let the curtain fall.